In Spite of the Consequences

IN SPITE OF THE
CONSEQUENCES

Prison Letters on Exoneration, Abolition, and Freedom

LACINO HAMILTON

Broadleaf Books

Minneapolis

Print ISBN: 978-1-5064-8816-5
eBook ISBN: 978-1-5064-8817-2
Printed in China

Library of Congress Cataloging-in-Publication Data

Names: Hamilton, Lacino, author.
Title: In spite of the consequences : prison letters on exoneration, abolition, and freedom / by Lacino Hamilton.
Description: Minneapolis : Broadleaf Books, [2023]
Identifiers: LCCN 2022054967 (print) | LCCN 2022054968 (ebook) | ISBN 9781506488165 (hardback) | ISBN 9781506488172 (ebook)
Subjects: LCSH: Hamilton, Lacino—Correspondence. | Prisoners—Correspondence. | Judicial error—United States. | False imprisonment—United States. | Criminal justice, Administration of—Moral and ethical aspects—United States. | Prison abolition movements—United States.
Classification: LCC HV8665 .H34 2023 (print) | LCC HV8665 (ebook) | DDC 365/.7—dc23/eng/20221118
LC record available at https://lccn.loc.gov/2022054967
LC ebook record available at https://lccn.loc.gov/2022054968

Dedicated to Sarah E. Hunter and Marvin Sealy

CONTENTS

FOREWORD

Just as slavery was a defining fact of American life from the seven-
teenth to the nineteenth centuries, mass incarceration is a central
feature today. And just as the abolition of slavery was unimaginable
to most Americans then, a society with no prisons or police is difficult for people to wrap their heads around now. But try it—imagine
a world without prisons and police. What would we need to have
and to be in order for that to be remotely possible? When enough of
us become liberated from the dogma of incarceration, the presiding
algorithm of misbehavior = punishment = the cage, and the total-
izing logic of captivity and control, we might mobilize ourselves to
dive into the hard work of building a political movement to empty
the prisons and shut them down. We may look back—just as we look
back at slavery today—with astonishment and anguish as we realize
that the prison-industrial complex and the militarized police were a
miserable choice: it generated super-profits for a few while it vital-
ized white supremacy, ruined millions of human lives, devastated
social capital, destroyed whole communities, and diminished our
society overall. Slavery, "the peculiar institution," made cruelty cus-
tomary and torture conventional; everyone was forced to witness and
embrace it as such, or to shut their eyes tight as communities were
made more hard-hearted and hateful. Just as the abolition of slavery
liberated enormous energy toward a more generous and compassion-
ate social order, so will a world without prisons create the conditions
for a more just and decent community for all.

Lacino Hamilton adds this essential text onto the scale toward abolition. He has written a powerful book for our times—a collection of ideas and essays, reflections and interventions, that read like messages in a bottle tossed into a stormy sea from a distant desert island. Hamilton writes with both desperation and hope—desperation because he's been kidnapped and exiled, thrust into the tangled and savage gulag with no apparent pathway to liberty; hope because the bottle *might* reach a far shore, *might* be picked up by a distant stranger; the contents *might* be read and understood and prod the reader to action. You now have the bottle in your hands—you can read this illuminating and inspiring account of one person's fight for freedom. And you might just be spurred to action.

These letters map the growth and development of an abolitionist. They chart an evolving consciousness and a relentless spirit in pursuit of truth, recognition, repair, and justice. It's an immense and remarkable journey.

Lacino Hamilton is a tireless and powerful teacher. In his opening letter he assures his correspondent that there are no dumb questions. It's true—in an infinite and expanding universe our knowledge is finite, and not-knowing is the default for all of us much of the time. There are no dumb questions, but the deeper question worth pursuing is this: whose interests are served by your not-knowing this or that fact, or this or that piece of information? The US 2023 National Defense Authorization Act is $847 billion—more than the world's next nine defense budgets combined. That's over 65 percent of discretionary US dollars spent on the militarized budget. Meanwhile, over half a million people are unhoused in the US, one in ten adults is in "significant" medical debt ($195 billion of debt held by individuals), 63 percent of people in the US are living paycheck to paycheck, and almost 17 percent of American children live in poverty. And, of course, with under 5 percent of the world's population, the US cages 20 percent of the world's prisoners. It's in the interest of the powerful, the one percent, the ruling class to keep us all blind to the social reality we're swimming through.

So…if you don't know, now you know.

The goal is not to *reform* or compromise enslavement, subjugation, abuse, cruelty, persecution, avariciousness, exploitation, predation, and oppression—freedom is the proper horizon. The brilliant abolitionist Ruth Wilson Gilmore argues that abolitionists today, as abolitionists in the past, are required to change one thing: *everything*. This is because abolition, she explains, is not best understood as a deletion or an erasure, but rather as an act of "world-building." What kind of world would we need to build in order to have no slavery? No afterlife of slavery? No prisons or police? Everything would have to change. Everything.

We can applaud the "second chances" projects even as we note that most people who are caged never had a first chance. We can support the Innocence Project even as we note that people who committed crimes—even terrible acts—are still human beings, each with a spark of the divine and each worthy of love and life. We can read widely and study scholarly materials seriously even as we note that it's unacceptable and unprincipled to understand the actions and behaviors of human beings without listening systematically to how they understand their situations, how they make meaning, and how they explain themselves.

Lacino Hamilton offers a unique and powerful entry point.

—Bill Ayers

PREFACE

My name is Lacino Hamilton. I spent over half my life imprisoned due to Detroit Homicide Detective James Fleming and Wayne County Prosecutor Ruth Carter using serial jailhouse snitch Oliver Cowan to secure a conviction against me through fabrication of evidence and the withholding of information regarding a jailhouse snitch scheme used by and known to police and prosecutors to secure wrongful convictions.

In the scheme, men arrested and facing charges were kept months, and sometimes years, at 1300 Beaubien, Detroit's 1st Precinct, even though precincts in Detroit only hold people up to seventy-two hours. The same handful of men illegally kept at the First Precinct were used to falsely claim that people confessed to crimes while being held there. Oliver Cowan falsely testified that I confessed to killing my foster mother of more than fifteen years. Homicide detectives supplied Oliver Cowan with the information needed to fabricate purported evidence of confessions.

On September 30, 2020, acting on a motion filed by the Wayne County Prosecutor's Conviction Integrity Unit, a Wayne County Circuit Court judge dismissed the charges against me and vacated convictions relating to my foster mother's 1994 murder in Detroit, Michigan. After an almost twenty-seven-year struggle to prove my innocence, I am now listed on the National Registry of Exonerations, a project run by the University of Michigan Law School and the Michigan State University of Law.

I do not know how to put that struggle in words. It is so much more than teaching myself to write, writing over ten thousand letters praying for help, becoming an abolitionist, and an imprisoned frequently published journalist inside the prison. It is how I felt while transforming myself and becoming—I felt like my life was at stake. Because fifty-two to eighty years, which is what I served twenty-seven years of, is a death sentence. If not for Claudia Whitman, founder and CEO of NCCAN, attorneys Mary Chartier and Takura Nyamfukudza, Roots Action, and a real community effort from so many people who weighed in, I probably would have died in prison for a "crime" I am innocent of. But instead, I'm writing my first book.

When it comes to imprisoned men and women, it does not matter how exceptional the skill or talent may be, the outside world at large rarely creates space for these people to apply their abilities. So, my success at being published and consulted on social issues while imprisoned in large part led to this book.

There were strong suggestions I write a book about my life and the struggle to prove innocence. I was excited about the opportunity to do something I had dreamed of doing for years, but I did not want to write a book where I was the primary subject and prison conditions were secondary. Imprisoned men and women have been stripped of nearly all liberties, human dignity, and respect and are dependent on other stakeholders in the system to provide them with access, which they rarely do.

My goal with this book is to center the focus on the tragic human costs of imprisonment.

I did not teach myself how to write in order to contribute to building a society and world with prisons. While writing thousands of letters asking for help to prove my innocence, I discovered there were several thousand other imprisoned people doing the same—writing for their lives. And since writing was the only option I saw that was able to help me marshal assistance proving innocence, I pushed to write well in order to have my letters stand out. I wrote over ten thousand letters while imprisoned.

Despite possessing a GED prior to imprisonment, when I decided writing was going to be the principal vehicle to pursue my liberties, I could not write a grammatically correct sentence. So, I began the difficult process of self-educating. Early on I read whatever I could get my hands on, whenever and however. First, I lacked direction, pedagogical theory, and knowledge of practices. I was attempting to acquire as much information as possible so as to have something of substance and quality in my letters, hoping that would assist me with standing out from others doing the same. Ultimately writing became a way of protesting the intentional harming of imprisoned men and women.

My style (method) of writing has much in common with a "participant observer" and a cultural anthropologist who lives in a foreign culture to understand and describe life in the most authentic way possible. However, what I write about in this collection of prison letters is familiar to me. I developed a penologist's, criminologist's, and sociologist's perspective of prison due to extensive research and study, and that permitted me to step back and analyze many of my and others' experiences as they were taking place.

This collection of letters contains truths and insights about prisons, and the social world more broadly, that are generally suppressed. This collection of letters to family, friends, lawyers, supporters, and fellow prisoners are arranged to help shape and give language to critically understand prison beyond the obvious deprivations. I wrote as a form of political intervention, never value neutral or objective. In this regard, this collection of letters is not simply about raising awareness about prison conditions. The more we know about something, or the more we know period, the more power we have to weigh in and do something intentional if necessary.

The more I learned and became intentional in my writing, it became necessary to try and build understanding in an effort to mitigate the emotional and psychological harms of consistent interference with the fulfillment of human needs and the blocking of developmental energy unfolding spontaneously and constructively, which, no matter how much is written, remains irreducible to prose.

As I became even more intentional in my writing, I became an abolitionist. I could not always use abolitionist language and decided against revisions. Despite prison's heavy censorship, the goal was to aid in transforming people's consciousnesses, values, attitudes, and actions in order to develop a more humane, participatory, inclusive, needs-meeting, and effective response to harm—new ways of organizing social life to better meet needs and therefore decrease harm as much as possible.

This collection of letters is not filled with a lot of "what can be done to easily make the crisis go away" prescriptions. The letters reflect what was happening around me, and others similarly situated, and the immediacy of the situation.

Many of the letters had to be concealed, passed and read in secret, and smuggled out of the prison. I spent over ten years in solitary confinement and over ten years of maximum security placement. For seven years, I was designated as a security threat because my insights define the world and possibilities for human existence differently.

The modern state, in order to enable its role, has established an elaborate coercive and oppressive penal apparatus to micromanage people's lives. I hope you do not enjoy what you're about to read.

INTRODUCTION

This book, which consists of letters I wrote to family and friends over the course of more than two decades of incarceration, defies easy categorization. It is not just a book of theory on what is wrong with prisons and what might work in their place. It is a book showing how I tried to figure out in real time how to survive a fifty-two to eighty-year prison sentence for a crime I am innocent of and sharing those experiences with others. It blends personal narrative with criticism and analysis of the criminal justice system, criticism and analysis that illustrate and explore incarceration in ways traditional narratives on the subject do not—from the inside through lived experience. It is my hope that what you are about to read will challenge all your assumptions about power, social life, criminal justice, and what goes on inside of American prisons and serve as a catalyst for moving us closer to abolishing them.

Letters written to family and friends was not my first idea for a book. My first idea was grouping together some of what I thought were my most insightful essays about prison. However, those essays were discarded by prison officials. Just thrown away. "A mistake," I was told. It was only after I shared my frustrations with a friend that she conveyed how informative she found my correspondence and suggested that I consider turning letters written to her into a book. At first, I did not see how a compilation of random letters would create a coherent narrative. "They will," she insisted. "Do something different. I guarantee if others read the letters you wrote to me over the years, not to mention if you could retrieve letters you have written to others, whoever reads your book will see all this incarceration for what it really is." In fact, I hope readers come to a new awareness and begin to look more critically at the social situation that allows prisons in the first place.

Before I was incarcerated and began exploring the history of American law and the historical appearance of the American prison system, I used to, like a lot of other people, refer to the criminal justice system as broken. I have since changed my mind. It is daunting to acknowledge, but this country's massive use of prisons on a scale the world has never before seen offers testimony not of a broken system but one that is ruthlessly effective. The prison system as it stands now, disappearing more and more people, corroding and damaging the human personality, robbing people of their individuality and creativity, if not their humanity, is working according to plan: making social problems temporarily invisible to create the mirage that something has been done.

This interpretation is at odds, I know, with reformist notions of liberalism. The liberal political agenda has never included prison abolition. Liberals have mentioned the intentions of Quaker reform, they have talked about the harm caused by mandatory minimum sentencing schemes, and even acknowledge how the war on drugs drastically increased the number of people in American prisons, but they have never seemed concerned with the realities that make prison a central American institution.

The Founding Fathers, the majority of whom were lawyers by profession—men wealthy in land, slaves, manufacturing, or shipping—enshrined their political philosophy that the rich must, in their own interests, either control the government directly or control the laws by which the government operates. The government they were forming was going to do more than play referee between various competing interests. It was going to protect the rich from the poor since the

Founding Fathers estimated the rich would always be in the minority. The Founding Fathers were putting their billfolds on the scale when creating a new government of laws and order.

Today "law and order" is assumed to be both natural and necessary, but it was actually through the creation of laws that the new government would maintain a special kind of order: a disproportionate distribution of power and wealth. It's not by chance that the rich get richer and the poor get prison. Anyone who disrupts or who has the potential to disrupt that order would be reviled, harassed, or have the proverbial book thrown at them—punished to the full extent of the law. The Constitution was not simply the work of wise men trying to establish a decent and orderly society. It was the work of elites trying to maintain their privilege while giving just enough rights and liberties to ensure popular support.

The absence of slaves, women, and white men without property at the Constitutional Convention was not the result of a scheduling conflict. The Constitution was not written with their interests in mind. Nor was it a miswording eighty-eight years later when the Thirteenth Amendment to the US Constitution made prison the new Black (i.e., slavery):

> Neither slavery nor involuntary servitude, except as punishment for crimes whereof the party shall have been duly convicted, shall exist within the United States, or any place subject to their jurisdiction.

Yes, you read that correctly. The Thirteenth Amendment to the US Constitution did not end slavery, like most of us were taught in grade-school history class. The Thirteenth Amendment merely placed stipulations on who could own slaves—the state—and that instead of being confined to plantations, jails, prisons, probation, and parole would be the new form of control and domination. Read the Thirteenth Amendment again. Neither slavery nor involuntary servitude *except* as punishment for crime. Slavery went from cotton-picking slaves to constitutional slaves, from economic control and domination to social control and domination, from Blacks to anyone duly convicted of a crime.

Of course, one of the first questions that anyone just discovering this would ask is how could this be in America, the land of the free? Well, the elites that controlled the state, an agency of concentrated power, defined it as the legitimate and only authority for resolving conflicts and harms, the legitimate and only agency for responding to loss and trauma. Authority and agency that used to rest with the family and community. The state began treating conflict and harm as property, real estate that the state then appropriated for itself. Backed by superior weapons and organized force, the state called the shots. That is, made the laws. And since this administrative unit of the state is by nature a war machine, its response to breaking its laws is deprivation of time and space, exclusion, punishment-violence, and execution.

It is disingenuous, surely, for those that traffic in incarceration to affect surprise each time it is revealed that more and more people are being imprisoned, for longer periods of time, for many "offenses" that were previously resolved by the family and community, or that incarceration causes more harms than it supposedly prevents. I articulate in this book of letters how incarceration is not an accident. How it is not random in distribution or effect. Prison serves the exact purpose for which it was originally intended—to run roughshod over and control the groups not represented at the Constitutional Convention. People of color are disproportionately imprisoned, women are the fastest growing population of prisoners, and poor whites are showing up on more and more prison count sheets.

I also articulate in this book of letters what living inside a prison is really like, for example, how people entering prison are immediately stripped of individual identity; how this practice of forced mixing of age, ethnic, and racial groups can lead to feelings of being contaminated by undesirable fellow prisoners and to self-segregation and gangs; how a breakdown of the barriers ordinarily separating sleep, work, and play—which are in prison all conducted in the same place and under a single authority—breaks down the barriers preventing guards from becoming tyrants; how a denial of heterosexual opportunities induces fear of losing one's masculinity and therefore produces a dangerous brand of hypermasculinity; and how after incarcerated men and women have been subjected to unfair and excessive punishment and treatment more degrading than that justified by law they often come to justify actions which could not have been justified when committed. I articulate what is seldom said, if it ever is, because millions of people never think to turn to incarcerated men and women as a reliable source of information and news about what goes on inside American prisons. You will discover from reading this book that they should be.

I suppose there are some people who truly are surprised because the sources they turn to for information and news almost universally project ideologically selected images of who is incarcerated and what the reasons are. These images have to be true if they are on the news, if they are shown over and over again, if they are preceded by the word "official," right? Wrong. The sources most people turn to for information and news often present a warped image of American prisons. As a consequence, millions in our country remain ignorant of tools besides coercion and violence to resolve conflict and harm, pain, and suffering.

Studying American culture and law in an effort to hold on to my sanity and acquire tools for survival, I learned that the stage is set for more of the same—even though the American public is assured by both major political parties that prison reform is coming. How do we reform something that is not broken? We don't. Reform is a ruse. We work to abolish prisons. We demand initiatives exhorting the community and society at large to respond differently to interpersonal harm and, on a more ambitious level, exhort us all toward a restorative culture, one of the most important paradigm shifts that could ever happen.

What the prison system needs is not reform, but vision, seeing justice not primarily as the infliction of pain and revenge through the imprisonment of the wrongdoer but essentially the restoration of fractured and broken relationships. The process will be complex, requiring a remarkable kind of moral and collective leadership that challenges, invites, and rewards greater participation. This book of letters is a contribution to that vision and part of that process.

I

Dear Dr. Fardan,[*]

No question you ask me is a dumb question. If you don't know, you are supposed to ask. Besides, what do you have in your personal experiences to size up the insanity of leading an enclosed, formally administered round of life?

I am certain you are aware that when one is sentenced to prison they have fallen far out of the social order. I am not certain if you understand just how far though? I should have asked you long before now, but do I ever give you the impression that, despite the obvious pains associated with having my life so rigidly structured, I am fine? Does the fact that I channel so much of my anger through essays and other literary mediums and not "acting out" conceal that the state has taken almost everything that can be taken? Does it conceal the difficulty of being sane in an insane place? Does it?

Imprisonment is not just the concrete, razor wire, bulletproof glass, or trained assassins watching from gun towers. Imprisonment is not just the isolation, monotony, loneliness, or assiduous misery. It is not just the anxiety, idleness, apathy, or pent-up frustration with nowhere to go (so it's usually internalized and you can guess the outcome of that). Neither is

---

[*] Professor of Sociology at Bowie State University, and founder of the Sojourner Truth Farm School, who became a longtime pen pal of Lacino's.

3

imprisonment just having to always chase after something, always having to hide something, or always having to hold my ground against something or someone. Imprisonment is also knowing how very different my life could have been. It is a perpetual defeat of sorts.

Imprisonment is the unimaginable reality that I, or anyone for that matter, can be kidnapped, held hostage, and divorced from habits, routines, and the familiar, normal, and regular activities of making a life. Such as a career. Who knows? Perhaps I could have become a literary success. A family, pleasant memories. Not the ones I've accumulated. There could have been significant contributions. It is the forceful, abusive, and violent manner in which prison policies, procedures, and programs assault my individuality and independence. Imprisonment is an asphyxiation of sorts.

Imprisonment is the systematic application of the principles of behavior modification. It is the techniques that include both rewards and deprivations you and others ordinarily expect not to have to sustain. It is the similarity between the prison and Dr. Frankenstein, whose diseased ego created a huge, pathologically strong, demented, ugly creature (re: prisoners). A creature that was functionally censored by making him underintelligent, erecting barriers flexible enough to keep him working but rigid enough to forestall any growth of his mental faculties. And like Dr. Frankenstein's monster, I am supposed to live through the master, which in this case is the prison. I am supposed to be content watching the prison flourish while I deteriorate. Imprisonment is a horror story of sorts.

Imprisonment is not just the cruel distance between family and me, friends and me but the disdain from prison staff to whom I am in close proximity. Imprisonment is the idea that if prison staff do anything other than give me commands, I will pose a danger. Imprisonment is prison staff who are under no obligation to maintain standards of humane treatment. I mean, there are standards, but there is no one here to enforce them. Imprisonment is the contradiction between what prison staff do and what prison websites and paid spokespeople say they do. Imprisonment is even when I am right, I am told I am wrong. Penalized if I do not agree that I am wrong. Imprisonment is a schizophrenia of sorts.

Imprisonment is the systematic process of reinforcing the fact that I have minimal control over the regulation and orientation of my own body. Imprisonment is the misleading name given to this condition: learned helplessness. A derivative of psychologist B. F. Skinner's operant conditioning called learned techniques. It is being forced to accept without question prison staff's efforts to control me. Imprisonment is a brainwashing of sorts.

Imprisonment is my talents under siege. Imprisonment is having my aspirations of being a public figure reduced to ruins. Imprisonment is dreams deferred. It is tomorrow and never today. It is days turning into weeks, which turn into months, then years, and getting lost in the confusion of it all. Imprisonment is a twilight zone of sorts.

Imprisonment is articles and not actions. Imprisonment is encouragement to accept rather than resist all this pain and misery. Imprisonment is always being told to be good. Always being told to use cunning and guile. It is being encouraged to shuck and jive. It is an encouragement to be a willing participant, an action so heinous as to give the word betrayal a favorable facelift. Imprisonment is doing everything I can to remain sane through the insanity of it all.

Imprisonment is a choice society has made. A choice in desperate need of rethinking. In desperate need of transformation. I have thought deeply about this and have numerous critiques and solutions I'd like to share with you, if you are interested?

Lacino

5

Dear Lisa,[*]

I wish there was some sort of family and friends of prisoners handbook available to answer the questions and concerns you have. Not only would it be a great resource for you, but I assume such a book would help the millions of people who struggle to understand and support someone in prison. Perhaps policy makers and prison administrators would read it also. They have the most to learn. But let me get to your questions.

When your brother last wrote to me, he expressed feeling (justified or not) that he has been deserted by associates and betrayed by those closest to him. He did not specify you or anyone in particular, but that is how he feels. Prior to entering prison, he had dozens of daily interactions. Now he only occasionally speaks to you and one of his children's mothers. I have tried to explain to him that as painful as it may be for him to accept, life continues in his absence. He told me it's as if he no longer matters; as if he never existed.

On the first day in prison, we receive a crash course in "leaving the world behind." Prison becomes a new world, with new rules and protocols. Everything is left on the other side of the gate, separating life and civil death. That is what prison is. Civilly we are dead. That is a humbling experience. Someone you do not know and have never seen before can make you get naked and show them the crack of your ass. They can make you "shut the fuck up." Make you divulge all your personal business, and replace your identity with one given to you by the prison. Humbling may be an understatement.

Suicide enters the minds of most prisoners at one time or another while serving their sentences, even short ones. Not everyone gets to the point where they write out a suicide letter, but the hopelessness of the situation, the constant agony and despair and frustration, produces a pain more excruciating than anything that can be inflicted on the body.

---

[*] The sister of someone with whom Lacino was incarcerated.

I have been there myself. I did not think about hanging myself or slitting my wrist, but on the second anniversary of being locked up, I just could not imagine fifty more of the past two years. As difficult as it is to escape, I thought it was better to die trying.

One positive is your brother is emerging from the deep depression he has been in. He is giving up his emotionally taxing efforts at anonymity. For months he rarely left the cell and talked only when it was absolutely necessary. Now he goes to the gym three times per week and attends Protestant service on Sunday mornings. It may make you feel better to know that his desire to stay to himself and out of contact is a phase most prisoners pass through. It's an attempt to avoid ratifying any interaction that presses a reciprocal role upon him and opens him to what he observes in the men around him.

For someone entering prison, the things they see must look like an episode of *The Walking Dead*. About 40 percent of the prisoner population is high off psychotropic medication. An even greater percentage is running around in acute confused states, experiencing ego dystonic aggressive fantasies. The assaults and stabbings have gotten really bad in the last few years. That's less of a criticism of prisoners (but it is a criticism) and more of an indictment of the level of abject deprivation and want in prison.

Do not be alarmed if he takes on a new nickname. It will probably be something you would not associate him with. I haven't figured it out, but I think taking a nickname is a disassociation mechanism. I think it's a way of shielding the person they were prior to prison from the person they are forced to become. Sort of like a "can't beat them, join them" attitude. Guys take on nicknames like Dirtbag, Cell Search, and Half-Dead.

A nickname is a sign of settling down into the new role as a prisoner. A sort of "coming out." You have to do your part to remind him that he isn't what the prison forces him to become. Plenty of letters, plenty of pictures, as many visits as you can schedule, opening up your life and experiences to him so he can live with and through you, never make him

feel guilty for things he has no control over, and push him to create opportunities where there appear to be none. And if he ever springs a dumb
nickname on you, ignore that. This may be the only time I encourage you
to ignore something your brother says or does, but do not reinforce any
harmful coping mechanisms he comes up with.

There is no way for me to respond to your questions in one letter.
Each question probably deserves several letters devoted just to it. Nothing that administrators and guards do is as simple as this or that. The
same for prisoners. There are some commonalities, but you are going to
have to wear a lot of different hats in order to assist your brother while he
is in prison and when he is finally released. A lot of what this experience
is doing to him will not be fully pronounced until he is released. We will
continue this, okay? I look forward to receiving your next letter.

Sincerely,
Lacino

Mary, Takura*:

I received the legal brief you and the rest of the team prepared on my behalf. I read it immediately. Then I read it again. You all did excellent work emphasizing all the critical contradictions and lies. Just remember, legal precedents and facts are not our problem; it's convincing people that are paid to put the reputation and legitimacy of the police and courts above people like me that they should do just that. Selling our position will require tremendous effort. It is a crapshoot. I would feel better if we had a pair of loaded dice.

When this nightmare began, I saw detective James Fleming and professional jailhouse witness Oliver Cowan as the shining examples of why the police and courts should be abolished. To some extent I was wrong about that, in that I overestimated their roles and the severity of the situation that made me their adversary. I have since tried to analyze and enlarge my understanding of what went down and why.

I had been focusing primarily on the piss-poor morals of detective Fleming and Cowan's crab-in-a-barrel mentality. I was focusing primarily on individuals instead of the situation. In fact, the more I understand the situation, as despicable and cowardly of an act it was for Cowan to take the stand in court and bear false witness against me, when someone facing a mandatory prison sentence is asked to cooperate in exchange for leniency, they almost always choose to do so. They have something very important at stake—their freedom. A very powerful incentive to lie.

In the minds of many people dangling in the grips of the police and courts, cooperation has become synonymous with hope. Pitiful, isn't it? No one wants to go to prison. If given the opportunity to avoid it, most will take it. Especially since the passing of more and more mandatory minimum sentences. Prosecutors regularly bribe vulnerable people, people who are at their mercy, with lenience in exchange for testimony

---

* Lacino's attorneys, working pro bono.

against others—even if it is not true. Prosecutors want convictions, not justice.

Lenience in exchange for testimony is not new. There have always been people who find themselves in compromised positions that have shifted the blame to lessen the consequences. But as far as who goes to prison and for how long, mandatory minimum sentences were a game changer. Prior to the late 1970s and early 1980s when Congress passed hundreds of harsher sentencing laws, judges possessed latitude when determining the length of time someone would be incarcerated or whether incarceration was warranted at all. This does not mean judges weren't harsh—they were. But they became harsher, raising the stakes for people facing incarceration and increasing incentives to become an appendage of the police and courts. In the vernacular, a snitch.

Opportunistic prosecutors who are graded on a win/lose scale make no apologies for holding mandatory minimum sentences over the heads of men and women who are routinely overcharged to begin with. Then they bribe them with lenience if they help them put another case in the win column. Prosecutors insist they are defenders of civil liberties, but on that score rests an unavoidable contraction: how can prosecutors rig the system with severe penalties for leverage and be defenders of civil liberties at the same time?

While courts have been reluctant to push back, because convictions go in the win column for judges too, there are numerous court decisions (seldom followed) that acknowledge the inherent unreliability of bribing someone with freedom or civil death. That is what courts consider incarceration—civil death. And prison administrators and guards have the gall to question the intensity of my fight for exoneration and release. I often wonder what they would do if it were them, civilly dead?

One judge wrote as he was leaving the bench that the use of people engaged in crimes to investigate and prosecute others suspected of criminal activity is fraught with peril. The hazard is a matter of urgency; they resort to sources "whose accuracy cannot reasonably be questioned."

Another judge wrote that never has it been truer that a person charged with a serious crime understands that the fastest and easiest way out of trouble with the law is to cut a deal at someone else's expense and to purchase leniency from the government by offering testimony that makes the government's case. Still, despite the recognition that such testimony is unreliable, courts permit it on the grounds that cross-examination will fetter out the truth. It's despicable, I tell you.

People who know little more about the police and courts than what they see on shows like *Law & Order* probably believe the police usually apprehend the right person and that they receive quality legal counsel, which forces prosecution witnesses to tell the truth. But if it were not for advances in DNA technologies and the hard work of those who advocate for innocent people, over four thousand people in this country would either still be in prison right now or dead because of the death penalty. Those are just the people who have been found to be wrongly convicted in the last couple of decades. As you pointed out in the legal brief, half of all wrongful convictions have been traced to false informant and jailhouse testimony, like Cowan.

But opportunistic informants and jailhouse witnesses do not generate wrongful convictions just because they lie. After all, lying testimony hardly distinguishes these witnesses from others. Police, prosecutors, medical examiners, they all lie. Rather, it is how and why informants and jailhouse witnesses lie, and how prosecutors depend on their lies and purchase those lies with leniency, that should be of issue.

For example, during my research I came across Leslie Vernon White of California. He faked confessions in dozens of cases, worming details about cases out of police and prosecutors over the phone while he was being held in the county jail. In 1991 Darryl Moore of Chicago, a professed contract killer, was paid cash plus given immunity from prosecution for a contract murder in exchange for testifying against three men. One of which died shortly after he was convicted. One received life in prison. And one received the death penalty. Later, Moore admitted that not only did he give false testimony, but he knew nothing of the crime for which the three had been convicted. Cowan is one of thousands of people whose vulnerabilities have been weaponized by the courts and police against people like me.

As weak, contemptible, and reprehensible as I find Cowan, he too was a victim. The man was dying of HIV/AIDS and facing a mandatory minimum sentence. The police and prosecutors used those vulnerabilities and weaponized that man. Cowan's false testimony was a shotgun blast to my young life—civil death. I was nineteen when he shot me with his lies. I am forty-three today.

Before I enlarged my understanding, I was not penetrating deeply enough. I was not focusing on the situation that weaponized the vulnerabilities of people like Cowan. That weaponizes winning. I am less angry at Cowen and angrier at the real issue, the imbalance of power that pervades all of American society. The power to weaponize one vulnerable person and civilly murder another.

A philosopher might analyze this process and prove, technically, that it is comic. But it is hardly ever funny.

Lacino

Dear Comrade,

I would greatly appreciate it if you never apologize for interactions between you and me that do not go well if there was no malicious intent. You are there and I am here. Worlds apart. Quite naturally there will be some misunderstandings, delays, other priorities. I get it. That's life. Besides, I learned years ago to distribute blame to those that deserve it. It is the state at fault.

When we enter prison, we do so with a conception of ourselves made possible by social arrangements (e.g., family, friends, neighborhood, work, relationships, a myriad of experiences) in our home world. Upon entrance we are immediately stripped of the support provided by those arrangements. Literally stripped butt naked. Our street clothes are taken and replaced with a prison uniform. Our name is changed to a prison number. Mine is 247310. The things we liked to eat or drink, the places we frequented, the activities we did for recreation, all of that is gone. We cannot see our family and friends if the prison says we can't. And even if the prison says we can, they still decide when and for how long.

These are not superficial abasements, degradations, humiliations, or profanations. They are the beginning of a perpetual process of radical shifts in the beliefs we have about ourselves and the world around us. The barriers prison places between this world and the one you live in do more than keep us in or keep you out; it disrupts how options are assessed, how decisions are made, and how estimations of what's possible, or not, are calculated, a disruption of the usual relationship between the individual actor and his or her acts.

In music a producer samples a song by taking three or four seconds or bars of a song, then putting it on a "loop," where those three or four seconds or bars play over and over. The entire song being sampled is not heard, only a small portion. The prison practices this same looping method. Except instead of producing a hit song, it produces a defensive response on our part.

The goal of the prison is control. Not just physical control but reducing prisoners to active accomplices or passive recipients of oppression—by making us believe we deserve what the prison dishes out. So, the stripping process isn't just taking our belongings but obliterating our conception of ourselves. Whoever we were or thought we were prior to prison, whether that was father, son, brother, husband, janitor, driver, or business owner, and especially if we thought we were some kind of "bad ass" or a combination of these and other identities, is stripped so that we can begin to see ourselves as a prisoner. This despicable thing. Nonperson. Object worthy of oppression.

This is where looping comes into play. Seeing ourselves as a prisoner means our entire world is collapsed into the assault, the murder, the burglary, the theft, the rape, whatever it is one has been sentenced to prison for. That is what we become and nothing else. The offense is placed on a loop and played over and over again, which places us on perpetual defense, always having to say sorry, beg for forgiveness, and swear we have changed no matter how long ago the offense occurred. It's the only way privileges are granted, and eventually a release if one is so lucky.

Think about something you have done that you are ashamed of, or at least not proud of. We all have done things we aren't proud of. Sit with that thought for a minute. What if every time anyone interacted with you, that shameful thing would be the only thing that came up? Not that you are a son, a husband, a father, an intellectual, a member of your community, just the thing you are the least proud of? That is precisely what happens in prison.

I am aware guards do not know if I am innocent or guilty, so I won't go down that road. But it's common knowledge among guards that my study regimen is sort of a legend in the penal system. They know I have published numerous essays. They know that I interact with several universities. They know after more than two decades of incarceration, I have no violence in my prison jacket, only educational accomplishments that have been scratched out of the terrain, guerilla style. But still, all of that is collapsed back into the offense I was sentenced to prison for. And not only is that supposed to justify the ways in which they attempt to contort my mind and body to fit into this tiny, tiny space, but I am supposed to be a willing participant. And looping doesn't end when the prison sentence ends.

Once a person has been in prison, the offense they went in for is the event that defines them and justifies denying them housing, employment, voting rights, safety net benefits, and any kind of respectable social standing. In many ways, God is the only entity that is forgiving. Society does not forgive, and the prison definitely doesn't because that would require seeing something redeemable in us. When there is something redeemable in someone, you treat them differently. You treat them like a human being, not an object. And the prison can't do that because the prison must operate efficiently, and it operates most efficiently when prisoners become accomplices in their domination and control.

I have to go for now. The guard will be at the cell shortly to escort me to see the doctor. But when you write back, I would like to explore why people who leave prison are more damaged than when they went in. And when they leave, they return to neighborhoods that have not substantially changed. This is another form of looping—environmental looping. But we will have to save this for another time.

Live not Memorex,
Lacino

Rhonda,*

If and when you make contact with the esteemed University of Michigan professor, please convey that my intention is to open a fluid line of dialogue in the hopes that she and I can find more effective ways to challenge some of the more flagrant and harmful practices of the criminal justice system. All this incarceration will not be eliminated until people who have privilege feel obligated to make the problem of caging people their own problem and to do something about it.

That means, in part, people like her, with influence and access to resources, building alliances with people like me, who are without, who are stigmatized and ostracized. It means people like her and people like me seeing what positions we share and where opportunities exist to work together. And if opportunities do not exist, doing something to create them. From the things she has written, it is obvious she recognizes incarceration in this country as a problem. But when a problem is recognized, it is irresponsible to leave it to others to take all the risk and do all the work.

She probably doesn't realize it, which is why my letters have gone unanswered, but it is a small victory for her and me to just have conversations about race, gender, socioeconomic status, what we think justice should look like, and so on, because there are so many barriers purposely constructed to prevent us from doing so. This is what I need you to get across to her. An open line of dialogue is a first step, a tool, if you will, for understanding what's going on and what incarceration has to do with all of us. Dialogue opens new ways of thinking about what appears to be common sense but is actually part of dynamic and complex social processes.

I don't take it personally when people do not respond to my requests to collaborate to do something about injustice and unnecessary suffering,

---

* A pen name for his girlfriend at this time.

and you shouldn't either. My responsibility is to not give up. To not get stuck in a kind of paralysis that perpetuates the trouble and its human consequences. Sometimes that means continuing to reach out to people who have shown no interest in reaching back out to me. It isn't good enough to simply say "I tried," then move on. My primary goal is to change how people think about incarceration. I have been less concerned with how many times I have tried to connect with others, and more concerned with the resilience and the fortitude to, in the words of my mother, "keep on keeping on." Thank you for helping make that possible.

Sincerely,
Lacino

Carl,*

I have a question for you: Do you think it is possible that you believe everyone is aware of what is going on in society just because you are? I think you and others make this crucial error in judgment all the time. A lot of people do not know much about events that do not directly impact food, clothes, and shelter, which means as much as you and others want everyone to "get down to it," education is likely going to precede action.

You have to be kidding (at least I hope you are) to say that most people know the story of the transformation of urban labor markets, particularly in older Rust Belt cities of the Northeast and Midwest. Where do you propose they learned this, in public school? From the pulpit? The media? Most people cannot tell you their own family history, let alone something as not so obvious as urban transformation and economic dislocation.

I grew up in one of those cities (Detroit) and did not know. I am not unique in that. It took me years of mining through books and learning how to watch the news and which publications to subscribe to before I began to catch on. And I would argue that despite advances in technology people have less general education today than they did just a couple of decades ago.

The first misconception is that jobs began drying up or being shipped overseas after the North American Free Trade Agreement (NAFTA) was signed into law in December 1992. Not true. Beginning as early as the 1940s and 1950s, in some cities like Detroit, Cleveland, and Pittsburgh, automotive and manufacturing industries began to deteriorate. As many as a million jobs were eliminated in the twenty years before NAFTA.

The second misconception is that the transformation of urban markets was a natural process. Supposedly companies grow, technologies

---

* Someone incarcerated with Lacino. He would write letters to him, even if they were in the same facility, because when on lockdown they might not be able to speak in person even if only thirty feet apart.

advance, then companies move to bigger (more exploitable) markets. Not true. Every one of these steps was shaped by political forces, federal investment in things like roads and highways and in the laying of fiber optics for the transmission of data at high speeds and in large amounts, governments legislating tax breaks and loopholes exclusively for companies and corporations, the relaxing of bank regulations, massive corporate subsidies, diplomatic marriages, and the use of the military to control international trade routes, governments, resources, and foreign markets.

The third misconception is that urban decline is just a story about the economy. Not true either. While many urban areas (where the majority of people of color are concentrated) experienced a rise in violence, hopelessness, and blight, surrounding suburbs fared quite well. Part of this narrative is a changing urban economy within the context of racial hostility, racial violence, political and demographic change, and unequal investment in populations and places.

I was arguing with a guy a few cells down a few weeks ago. He was of my grandmother's generation and swore up and down that Mayor Coleman Young, Detroit's first Black mayor, ruined Detroit. I tried to get him to understand that when whites fled Detroit for the surrounding suburbs, it did not alter the fact that they still held the bulk of economic power in Detroit. Furthermore, whites that fled could still vote in the state legislature and have a direct impact on the city of Detroit—and they did. It only looked like Mayor Young and an all-Black city council was running Detroit. In reality, the economics of the city were controlled by the surrounding suburbs, and policy was controlled by the state legislature.

The fourth misconception is that whatever the problem is, we should blame it on absent fathers or the myth of noncaring mothers. The guy a few cells over tried to convince me of this just yesterday when discussing the trash problem on the eastside of Detroit.

He did not understand that it is not the job of absent fathers or so-called noncaring mothers to collect trash; it is the job of the department of sanitation. It had not occurred to him that regardless of their home situation, there are public services to which all residents of Detroit are entitled. Ridiculing people for not becoming trash collectors while trying to keep the rent up and food on the table is diabolical.

The most disturbing implication of this sort of ridicule is that uncollected trash reflects defects in the home. In effect, presenting an apology for social neglect and abuse.

The truth is, most people know little of what does not impact their day-to-day struggle for survival. Not because they are stupid, as some would lead us to believe, but because they are purposely kept ignorant. If a person does not know much, they cannot do much. And that there is the goal: to have a population of neglected and abused people who cannot do much about it.

There is no law in the universe that says schools cannot teach students (from the earliest grades) about the economics and politics directly impacting their lives. There is nothing preventing the media from using its vast resources to give a minute-by-minute update of changes to laws and their intended impact, the same way it reports on the lives of men and women who are famous for little more than being famous.

It is easy to say we want action right now and perhaps strike a limited blow that will be explained away as deviance. It is another thing to build slowly and build quality. To cultivate solid bonds constructed on substance and in sincerity. To facilitate the acquisition of knowledge and critical thinking skills, and not become discouraged by the obstacles and occasional setbacks that cannot be avoided.

Unfortunately, I have to end this here. I look forward to your response and ways we can expand this dialogue to a larger audience.

Your friend,
Lacino

Comrade,

You are right about Emmett Till's family not calling the sheriff when he was kidnapped from his relative's home in the middle of the night, beaten, and subsequently murdered. But you are right from a lazy perspective. It had nothing to do with his family being cowards, as you write. Though they probably did fear what might happen if they did, and with good cause, his family did not call the sheriff because in 1955 in Money, Mississippi, calling the sheriff was summoning the Ku Klux Klan. And what sensible Black family would do a thing like that?

It is easy to say what you would have done back then. I hear it all the time how someone would have scaled a wall, jumped over a snake pit, declined help fighting a bear, stopped to help an old lady cross the street, eaten a can of spinach, then went Popeye on the sheriff. If we were talking cartoons, I might believe them. But in 1955 in Money, Mississippi, saying there was an imbalance of power between Blacks and law enforcement is a gross understatement. Blacks did not have to rule out calling the sheriff—it wasn't even an option. Calling the dogcatcher wasn't an option. Blacks developed communal ways to mediate interpersonal disputes and community conflicts that did not involve state actors.

There were no judges or juries or professionally trained negotiators. Just people in the community who were respected for their knowledge (often that boiled down to lived experiences) and ability to be honest brokers who used a talking-out procedure to resolve conflict. When there was an injury or loss, they figured out what needed to be done to repair or make up for the injury or loss—and what could be done to prevent it from happening again. There was no turning people over to law enforcement to deal with members of the community how they saw fit. They knew, the same way we know today, that when law enforcement gets involved, the interest wasn't going to be resolving conflict or repairing injury or loss. There was probably going to be more injury and more loss, like never-being-seen-again-type loss.

I point to this when people tell me that professional law enforcement is a necessary part of human society. That's not true. This wasn't just Money, Mississippi. This was Black communities in both the North and South, examples of the human ability to solve problems in a nonviolent and nonauthoritarian way. It shows that communal problem-solving works. You have the resources, check for yourself, this whole adversarial, retributive-style justice was imposed on Black communities. And in case no one has noticed, it has not resulted in better, safer, or more livable communities. Actually, just the opposite has occurred.

What we need is not strategies to deal with people who harm others. Because if you do some of that research you tell me so much about, the harmer has usually been harmed him- or herself. That's what happens— hurt people hurt people. We need to target the places where harm occurs and is usually concentrated. Make those places better. Invest in the places people live. Humanize those places as part of a process of us being more human.

I really wish there was more time to develop this line of thought. The people here are tossing cells, and the one I am in is next. I know I will be in a foul mood when I come back to the cell and will not feel like writing. I do not have much, but it is mine and I do not appreciate when guards come in here and throw my things around like they or I don't matter.

Just remember that because social experiences are one way now does not mean they have always been that way or will stay that way forever. Social experiences can change, and we can be out in front of that change.

Rebuild,
Lacino

Mom & Dad,

Why would you write me something like that? Alzheimer's? Neurosis? Some form of psychosis? Please tell me that is what it is. Anything but that you believe I should wait passively for the state to admit I was wronged. Because that's not going to happen. How many times do I have to share with you to never advise, hint at, or suggest that being good will somehow better my situation?

What exactly do you mean by that? Following rules that denigrate me as a man, that treat me like a child, that require me to surrender my dignity and self-respect? Rules that forbid me from openly questioning the legitimacy of the state's authority to incarcerate me? Rules that severely censor alternative ideas about power? I keep writing to you, trying to tell you that ideas are something I have to spare. Seventeen years' worth of ideas.

I possess no illusions about the possibility of radically changing prison simply by advocating for social justice and human rights. However, I do feel strongly that advocating for them within prison has a place in the broader social justice and human rights struggle: Ohio, Lansing, Tunisia, Egypt, Libya. Social justice and human rights are ideas inspiring populations all over the earth. Struggles that are becoming more varied.

I do wish you were on the right side of history. Or at least on my side. I could teach the two of you. You are not too old to contribute in significant ways. That is the beauty of what I am part of. Principles trump politics, and people are valued over profit. That hope-starved, resource-strapped neighborhood you live in, largely bounded by schools that do not teach, where unemployment and despair run wild, could be the next capital. Options for support will not be limited to what can be hoaxed, stolen, or snatched. And you will not have to cede the streets to deviant behavior.

I have not been idle the past seventeen years. I have painfully educated myself to the point where my vision is clear and my ability to endure pain is astronomical. I will never again allow anyone to move on me without having first- and second-strike capacity. I am not waiting on some super negro to fly in and save the day. We must save ourselves.

I could be sitting in your living room tomorrow if you would stop listening to those frauds and charlatans that come on TV late at night trying to convince you to finance their American dream. I could be there with you tomorrow if you would put your faith in the people and politics we address. But I love you just the same. I have nothing, so I have nothing to lose.

Your son,
Lacino Darnell H.

P.S. If for some reason I do not make it out of here alive, do not send for my body. Save your money, flowers, and tears. My work and life are not in vain. What you do not understand, future generations will.

Dear Rhonda,

I'm taking a break from writing the preface to my suicide letter to the Michigan parole board. I was about four or five paragraphs in, but it isn't flowing the way I'd like. If you don't mind, perhaps I can work out some of the language and overall structure by writing to you first? I've always found it easy to express myself to you.

When my nosy cellmate looked over my shoulder and saw the title of the preface, he freaked out. "What is a preface? Are you really going to kill yourself? Don't do it, you like the strongest person I know." His concern was making me more scared and nervous than him.

After I calmed him down a bit, I explained what I was writing and why. I shared with him that a preface is a preliminary statement, usually in a book, written by the author or editor setting forth the book's purpose. Or in this instance, the purpose of my letter to the Michigan parole board. I emphatically assured him I have no plans of killing myself. Then I detailed for him how detective James Fleming and serial witness Oliver Cowan already had.

I explained how suicide is not just the intentional taking of one's own life but also the destruction of one's own interests or prospects, and that there is an unwritten but very well-known Michigan parole board policy that if a prisoner does not accept responsibility for the offense he or she has been convicted of, the parole board will outright deny parole. I'm not taking responsibility for something I did not do.

It does not matter if we have served decades, like I have, or if a prisoner has an exemplary prison record, the parole hearing will end the second one asserts innocence. And since I will never take responsibility for something that is as obvious as the nose on my face that I had nothing to do with, it "kills" my prospects of being granted parole—suicide.

Truth of the matter is, if a prisoner, so-called, takes responsibility or not (which amounts to more than saying I did this or that but repairing what has been damaged), the parole hearing will last no longer than five minutes, most of which time will be spent with the interviewer thumbing through a file, grunting, and sighing. I mean it is no stretch of the imagination to surmise that prior to the hearing, a decision has already been made to grant or deny parole. Still, assuming the parole board could be persuaded to grant parole, is five minutes enough time to demonstrate that I should be immediately released, with an apology, reparations, and a commitment to work with me to release the others? I wasn't the only one this happened to.

Is five minutes enough time to explain that there is no justifiable reason to arrest me? There was no physical evidence linking me to the offense. Is five minutes enough time to explain that after being arrested and placed in an isolation cell for five days, detectives never asked me one question? A practice so unusual that the dozens of homicide detectives consulted from different parts of the country all say that it never happens, not in a murder investigation.

Is five minutes enough time to explain that the entire case hinged on the testimony of a jailhouse witness? That is really a misleading term. I was in the precinct with the man who testified I confessed to him. The average stay in a precinct is forty-eight to seventy-two hours. He lived there for a minimum of seven months. A man I did not know from Adam. He alleges he was sweeping and I stopped and told him my entire life story (police records prove his timeline of events did not and could not have happened). Recently discovered police records reveal that Oliver Cowan and Joe Twilley, another serial witness, together testified in over thirty (30) murder cases alleging to have received unsolicited confessions at the precinct. Serial witness Joe Twilley lived at the precinct for three years.

Is five minutes enough time to explain that serial witness Oliver Cowan testified I confessed to him three or four days after I was arrested, even though precinct records prove he was with detective James Fleming just hours after I was arrested, signing a fabricated statement saying I confessed? Is it enough time to explain that three new witnesses have come forward? One who knows the real perpetrator. One who was present when detective James Fleming gave serial witness Oliver Cowan a prewritten statement to rehearse and say I confessed. And one who admits detective James Fleming tried to pressure him to give false testimony against me, also.

Is five minutes enough time to ask for the opportunity to show the parole board a recently discovered internal memorandum from the Wayne County Prosecutor's Office naming serial witness Oliver Cowan, admitting he was part of a small cadre of jailhouse witnesses illegally living at Detroit's First Precinct for months and years and suspected of fabricating testimony in exchange for "illegal favors and leniency"?

Is five minutes enough time to explain that according to Northwestern Law School's Center on Wrongful Convictions, 45.9 percent of documented wrongful convictions have been traced to false informant testimony, making jailhouse informants the single leading cause of wrongful convictions?[1] Or is five minutes enough time to explain how I have educated myself, some say to a PhD level, writing for national and international publications, with numerous employment opportunities awaiting me upon release? The parole board could release me right now, they could release thousands of men and women whose return to society would add tremendous value. But of course, five minutes is not enough time to explain one, let alone all of these critical factors.

July 2018 I will have served twenty-four years. The parole board seems to want to hear people say uncle and does not seem concerned with using its power to right an obvious wrong. Using its power to right a wrong that others have ignored, because they could do so if they wanted to. Parole boards have been given the power of life and death. The power of who has a second chance at life and who remains dead to the world at large.

I just came back from the prison counselor's office. I was informed the parole board will not be seeing me next month. I suppose I don't have to commit correspondence suicide; the parole board has decided to kill my opportunity to even meet with them. I am still going to complete and send the letter to them. When I do make it out, and it shouldn't be much longer, I don't want anyone saying they did not know or what they would have done had they known.

Now I just have to condense this a bit and get it in the mail. Thank you for helping me.

Lacino

Rhonda, Rhonda, Rhonda,

I rushed back to the cell after you left to get what I'm thinking out of my head and into this letter while everything is still near the surface. You are a beautiful woman, and I am not merely referring to everything being so perfectly proportioned or your eyes. I kept getting lost in them, as if I were seeing you for the first time. Damn, woman, I am talking about your beauty that everyone recognizes. But when I call you beautiful, I also mean I could listen to you speak even if you began repeating yourself or mumbling. Your rhetoric stirs my soul. Emphasizes your deep commitment to creating a better world. I love the way you think.

I have known since we were younger that you are fiercely independent and take enormous pride in saying and doing exactly what you want, when you want. Those are the qualities that first attracted me to you, that have allowed us to remain friends all these years later. You are just as rebellious as I am. But it is different when you are live and in the flesh rather than when I am reading it in a letter. When our individual orbits collide. I think that is what people mean when they speak of sparks flying or fireworks going off. All that when you strutted into the visiting room—all that.

I will be honest, I did feel a little uncomfortable when you walked through the door. As I looked around the visiting room, looked into the face of everyone visiting with their friends and loved ones, I could see the frantic attempts to figure out who you were there to visit. There I was thinking what everyone else was thinking—that women who possess all the attributes men itch for, attributes you possess in abundance, seldom make appearances in places like this. You are going to have to tell me how I came to be so lucky. I'm going to have to go do something to build up a sweat when I am through with this letter. Do something to disperse some of the energy still building even though you left over an hour ago.

But before I do, I would be remiss if I did not ask you to disregard the theatrics of prison. Visits are Hollywood performances at their best.

29

Both décor and conduct are closer to societal standards than are those that prevail in the actual housing units, almost night and day in terms of guards' manners and prison cleanliness.

Guards in the housing unit aren't as friendly as the guards assigned to work the visiting area. Actually, if those same guards were reassigned to the housing unit, they would go from friendly to not friendly at all. The visiting room is a fiction. As soon as you left and I stepped through those visiting room doors back into the real prison, I had to get naked, show both sides of my hands, raise my arms over my head, open my mouth and stick out my tongue, lift up my private parts, turn around, show the bottoms of both feet, and the most degrading and humiliating part is always left for last: "Bend over and spread them." What could the guard possibly be looking for?

The view that visitors get helps decrease the pressure that might otherwise be brought to bear on the prison. If our family and friends saw with their own eyes what prison is really like, they would be outraged. The visiting room provides an image that will minimize concern for us. This includes the image of prisoners in the visiting room who sweep, mop, take out the trash, and take pictures. Their loyalty to the prison is not a simple representation of the character of the entire prison population. Few prisoners are that cheerful, courteous, or clean. It's hell back here in the housing units. Everything, small things, mean so much more because the things needed the most are always in short supply.

I just want you to know these things in the event something I write or say to you does not match your experiences in the visiting room. Visits are a well-choreographed, dressed-up view of the misery in which I live. Okay?

Sincerely yours,
Lacino Hamilton

Dear Leslie,*

It is with a heavy heart and profound sadness that I extend condolences to you, your family, and all the people who were blessed to know the magnanimous woman Sarah† was. By virtue of her commitment to justice and tenacious efforts to perfect the rule of law, Sarah warrants the designation of historical figure. The consciousness that she possessed—that the pursuit of justice is a constant struggle—doesn't simply appear. From what she shared with me, it was something that grew over time and something she worked into.

Any other designation is to turn our back on one of the brilliant minds of her generation. An individual passionately involved with liberating all of us, not just the accused and convicted. Sarah was keenly aware that how society treats the least among us, a category those of us in prison qualify for, says a lot about society as a whole. Sarah was so much more than a lawyer.

You lost a sister, her daughter and son lost a mother, her nephew lost an aunt, and the legal community lost a constitutional warrior and a freedom fighter. But those of us who are incarcerated, those of us who really knew Sarah and her work, gained a martyr for the cause of justice, for fairness and the fair application of law.

Sarah was one of my first experiences with someone willing to strain with me simply because it was the right thing to do and because I needed help. In this hour of grief and heartache, I would like to offer wise counsel. You asked what you could do to help me. This is what I would ask.

No more thoughts, words, or work will be coming from Sarah E. Hunter. So, we now must micro-analyze her wisdom that we do have. You said her bed and office are covered with dog-eared books and notes, that she had begun writing a blog? Keep Sarah's desk, chairs, notes, anything

---

* A childhood friend of Lacino's.
† Sarah Hunter, an attorney and activist, a whistleblower on police and FBI corruption, who died by suicide.

and everything that belonged to her. This beautiful woman's thoughts, words, and work should be shared and live on after her personal life. That way we make her live forever.

See, it's not how she passed, nor whether she lived to be sixty or six hundred. How she lived and what she was passionate about most is what matters. It is the wisdom, help, and guidance that she left and that touched so many people that matters. That is what lives on. That is what we must carry on.

And if time and place do not favor such an endeavor, pack everything and keep it until I am released. It should not be much longer. I do not have it all figured out right now, but I will see to it her life and sacrifices are not forgotten.

Because she was a constitutional warrior and freedom fighter, and because she went up against such entrenched injustice, we cannot expect her to come out the same way she went into that fight. The fight for justice touches the mind, body, and spirit. Sometimes for the better. Sometimes for the worse. But because of Sarah's courage and strength, you and your family are not alone in the grief you feel. Sarah was a paragon and touched the lives of thousands of people. And she will live on through us.

Sincerely,
Lacino Hamilton

Dear S. De Areuso,[*]

Enclosed is a form rejecting the letter you recently mailed. There is a possibility I may be allowed to read but not possess your letter. That is to be determined at a later date when the mail rejection is reviewed with me by an administrator.

The Michigan Department of Corrections (MDOC) mail policy was made more restrictive last October supposedly to prevent the introduction of contraband into Michigan prisons. It places increased distance between incarcerated people and their family and friends.

Soon after most people are incarcerated, they become letter writers. I do not know a prisoner or someone in their family that does not write letters. Letters are the least expensive way to keep in touch. They are also the least immediate, but they are the lifeline for most prisoners.

I have had conversations with prisoners that have shared with me that letters are almost a requirement for their sanity. Yet some people in here do not receive any mail at all. I wonder if they are going insane.

Some prisoners are illiterate, and some of their family members are also, like my father. He dropped out of school in the third grade. Wits carried him through life. I imagine that when an incarcerated person and people who wish to support him or her are both illiterate that it is like being confined twice.

The exchange of ideas and feelings are not often expressed even when one can write well. This is self-censorship. All incarcerated people are aware that prison staff read letters going in and out of the prison. They say they pry into our lives like this to check for conspiracies or anything that could harm staff or other prisoners, but on a slow day a bored guard may read an entire letter. No one wants someone knowing their most intimate thoughts to someone else. That lessens the ease of writing. Incarcerated people are always on guard about putting what they want

---

[*] A pen pal of Lacino's from Australia

to say most to family and friends into letters. Because of this, spontaneity is lost.

It is it unlikely to happen, but if incarcerated men and women were permitted to participate in the crafting of mail policies, perhaps important things like this could be taken into consideration. If incarcerated people were consulted in an honest way, there would be far less opposition to rules.

Several years ago I tutored for the University of Michigan-Dearborn campus's Inside-Out Prison Exchange Program. At the beginning of each semester, inside and outside students would be asked what rules they think are necessary to facilitate an environment where learning can take place and where people will be respected. Whatever students come up with is written on huge placards. After input, discussion, and consensus, what is agreed on becomes the de facto "rules" of the class.

The rules were not one-sided, as some may assume. The university instructors and prison staff present were permitted to suggest, discuss, and vote too. There is a lesson in this: people are more likely, in or out of prison, to disregard rules they have no role in creating. When incarcerated people are not permitted to participate in processes that impact their lives, it intensifies their already profound sense of isolation, loneliness, and mistrust of prison officials' motives.

Implicit in this level of participation is the recognition of the human capacity to make final judgment in matters of right and wrong. A humanity-affirming model of justice.

Lacino

Dear Lisa,

My sister from another mother. I care about both you and your brother. That is why it pains me when you write things like you wish your brother was more like me, more capable of dealing with prison with dignity and like a man. I hope that is not the way you talk to your brother because he is a man. Never throw his manhood in his face because his information and strategies are not as refined as the prison's information and strategies. Prisons have over four hundred years of imprisonment and slavery to draw from. Over four hundred years of breaking backs, wills, and spirits in their repertoires.

Let me be clear. The man that I am today, with over fifteen years served on what is essentially a death sentence, is not the same man I was when I only had a few years in, like your brother has served. In the beginning, before I made prison a study of mine, I thought I was losing my mind. One of the most pervasively threatening things that can happen to someone, to feel like you are losing control of yourself and not knowing what to do about it. It is like having an out-of-body experience.

I spent a lot of time seeking advice from older prisoners who appeared to have a handle on things. That was a mistake. They gave me a lot of general advice, like to go to the law library, watch what crowds I keep, and read books. The advice was so general that it was meaningless. When someone is giving advice, it should be tailored to fit the individual and the particulars of the situation the individual is confronted with. I wasted a lot of time thinking the answers to my problems could be found in the law library, judging other prisoners by haphazard standards, and flipping through the pages of books that were not relevant to what was going on in my life.

No one enters prison prepared to rise above the strategic measures meant to force us to pledge allegiance to prison administrators and guards. I am talking about being compelled to stand at attention with hand over heart. Neither is anyone prepared to cope with what is essentially being a failure at being a human being; a failure at being anything that one could respect as worth being. A prisoner is bottom of the barrel. No one respects us. Those who are "prison prepared" are prepared strictly from the physical: prepared to fight and stab. Prepared to hurt others? Had any of us really been prepared, we would have put up way more resistance to entering prison. We would have embraced a "desperate times calls for desperate measures" mentality had we known the facts.

Regardless of how violent prison is or isn't, the experience of imprisonment is primarily an emotional and psychological experience. It is some real weird and sick science that created these places. Think not? Lock your children in the bathroom for years and see how you are portrayed. Weird and sick would be compliments. But that is what prison is, fantastically strange and diseased. I am actually locked in a cell smaller than the average bathroom. So is your brother. That is enough to produce a disintegrative reevaluation of oneself. That is not easy to accept.

The emotional and psychological alterations required to change so as to fit into such a small space are enough to make one feel like they are losing their mind. I know there has been a time in your life when you were making a concession to conform to your job or fit your lifestyle or even to suit a relationship and you thought to yourself, "I must be losing my mind," or said, "I have to be crazy," but went ahead with it anyway. Your brother, like a lot of other people in prison, probably constantly questions himself to the point where he does not know if he is losing his mind or going crazy. This can be extremely frightening. Especially when "being a man" consists of keeping everything on the inside and trying to cope with extremely high levels of stress and anxiety alone.

Your brother entered prison with an identity, relationships, and rights and lost them. This is what I mean by one feeling like one is losing control, and not knowing what to do about it. Yes, your brother still has you, and his nephews, but what about his identity, his rights, and all the other relationships he has been unable to hold on to? You are right, he is not the same person he was before he entered, and he will not be the same person when he exits. No one experiences something like this and comes out on the other side the same. But I am not saying that change has to be degenerative. Remember, I started off this letter saying that what made the difference for me is that I made prison a study of mine.

While the transition from society to prison brings a sharp decrease in adult free status, it commonly isn't until many years have been served (usually within the first three to seven years) that prisoners begin to cast their minds back over the sequence of steps leading to imprisonment and feel that a lack of offense was sustained while their long-range best interests were being undermined. They feel like they betrayed themselves.

At least a few dozen times a day, I hear someone say that when they get out, they are not coming back. That they will hold court in the street. That they prefer death right there on the spot. This is because now they know. This realization is a moral experience that further separates one from themselves losing their mind.

During slavery, what are called Negro Spirituals often had double meanings. The song that says, "O Canaan, Sweet Canaan, I am bound for the land of Canaan," often meant that slaves wanted to get to the North, their Canaan. During the Civil War, when many slaves had escaped to the North, they made up new spirituals with bolder and more overt messages. For example, "Before I'd be a slave, I'd be buried in my grave, and go home to my Lord and be saved." That is because they were aware of what imprisonment on plantations really meant, unlike their ancestors who were packed on slave ships headed for America 245 years earlier.

What you recognize as a difference in how your brother is coping with imprisonment and how I am coping with imprisonment is a difference in information and knowledge. Because I have studied criminology, penology, brainwashing (politely described as conditioning), behavior modification, the plantation system, bureaucracies as a system, and so on, I have been able to build a defense. I have stopped participating in and facilitating deprivations (best I can) that make life in here a living hell.

People in prison feel a lot of guilt for going along with what is happening to them. Especially the ones that counsel a strategy of patience, of acceptance of what so-called cannot be helped, and a strategy of survival that says, "Take what is given because one day things will get better," when there are no objective signs of that. Lisa, information and knowledge alone will not change your brother's condition, but it is a start to changing his mentality. The beginning of changing from submission to defense, and from defense to offense. You, his nephews, and everyone else who wish to support your brother also need proper information and knowledge so you can fight with him.

I will leave off here, for now. I am anxious to read what you think about this.

Your other brother,
Lacino

Dear Adrian,*

I received the money today, thank you. I cannot explain what your financial support means. Actually, "financial support" is an inadequate term. The money you send permits me to opt out of both the prison work system—which should not be thought of as work in the way it is thought of in the larger society—and opt out of hustling to meet my most basic needs. The money you send is self-esteem support, self-respect support, dignity support. So much more than a medium of exchange.

When you go to work, the job ends when you punch the time card at the end of your shift. Every two weeks you receive a paycheck, and with it you pay down bills, purchase services, and find something to get into that brings you some momentary release or pleasure. The work you do is essential to your life, but it's still just a part of your life. In prison the work has no cutoff point.

The guard I have been waiting on for the last hour to bring me some toilet paper, who I have to ask permission to use the phone, who strip searches me before and after a visit, who reads my incoming and outgoing mail, who tosses the cell once or twice per week, is also the boss. As much as you and millions of other people may dislike your boss, you don't have to deal with him or her after you punch that time card. In here it is different. The authority is seamless.

This seamless authority means, if I express displeasure with it taking so long to bring me toilet paper or if I wasn't polite enough when I asked permission to use the phone or if my body language conveyed my embarrassment when the officer commands, "Bend over and spread them,"—I mean the deference you show your boss, that everyone to some degree shows their boss, borders on sadomasochism in the prison setting. Imagine what life would be like if your boss controlled and dominated every aspect of your life. Okay, stop thinking about it because I know

---

* A childhood friend of Lacino's.

how frightening a thought that must be. Except that in prison it isn't a thought, it's a sick reality.

Equally as frightening is that the work is designed more to keep us busy than to add value to our lives. Have you ever heard of a "spoon roller?" This is a kitchen job where a team of about five or six people sit in a circle with thousands of spoons and paper napkins and they roll spoons into the napkins. Five or six men expected to roll seven thousand spoons per day. Talking among themselves breaks up the monotony, but the boss often instructs them to "shut up and roll."

In other cases, of course, more than a full day's hard labor is required, induced not by reward (the highest paying job in prison is $0.32 per hour) but by threat of punishment. If one does not work hard enough or fast enough, which are subjective, they will be fired, which means being sent back to twenty-three-hour lockdown to suffer extreme boredom. If one is fired and is written up for misconduct, that can turn into twenty-four-hour lockdown: loss of phone access, loss of commissary, solitary confinement, even having days added to our prison sentence. Working under these conditions turns work into a kind of slavery, with our labor placed at the convenience of guards. A sick reality.

Whether there is too little work or too much, the person who was work-oriented on the outside tends to become demoralized by the work system of the prison. This is why I say the money you send should be thought more along the lines of self-esteem support, self-respect support, and dignity support. In here, one's sense of worth and of pride can become alienated from their work capacity. And all that spiel about teaching work ethic, there isn't an administrator or guard willing to work under the same arrangements.

I mentioned the "hustling system" in the beginning of this letter and want to share with you the full meaning of that.

Hustling in or out of prison carries negative connotations. I mean, even if you just look the word "hustle" up in the dictionary, it says to push or knock about, shove or jostle in a rude, rough manner. But you know like I know, while hustling can and often does involve illicit activities, generally speaking, it just means creativity, initiative, and drive. Or as the old classic Tupac song says, finding a way to make a dollar out of fifteen cents.

Many people in society need both a job and a hustle to make ends meet. They use their skills, know-how, and creativity to bring in additional (or sometimes only) income. Some women do hair in their living room, prepare taxes, or babysit. Men who have auto mechanic skills might repair cars in their garage, build a desk on the weekend, or offer to pump someone's gas. All forms of hustling. In prison where jobs pay slave wages and there is always a shortage of everything, prisoners use their skills, know-how, and creativity to hustle up on the extras needed to get by.

Some prisoners repair appliances, do legal research and write legal briefs, run prisoner stores, wash and fold clothes, and provide dozens and dozens of other needed services. Unlike in society, where Uncle Sam may want to crack down on these "off the book" jobs because they want a cut of the money, in prison they are simply outlawed.

For example, the last time I sent my typewriter in for repair there was a $175 bench fee. With parts and labor, the repair totaled more than the actual purchase cost of the typewriter. The prison "fix-it guy" could have repaired it for five bags of coffee (i.e., $18). The cheapest appeals lawyer cost several thousand dollars. Jailhouse lawyers, most of whom have researched and studied law for decades, and sometimes know more than lawyers, do the same work for a few hundred dollars. And to a poor defendant desperate for legal assistance, a jailhouse lawyer is often the difference between legal help and no legal help at all.

Outlawing hustling in prison will not eliminate it, because the need for these services will not be eliminated. Instead, needed services become crimes, and prisoners are compelled to circumvent, manipulate, deceive, and outwit—frames of mind the prison purports to rehabilitate but actually promotes.

Prison officials are aware that there are needed services the prison does not provide. Instead of prison officials training prisoners in these services or setting up systems where they can be fulfilled without having to circumvent, manipulate, or deceive, the prison has criminalized creativity, initiative, and drive. And after spending years circumventing, manipulating, and deceiving, it's not a stretch of the imagination to think this frame of mind would be taken back to society upon release.

And it's not just hustling. If a friend got word to me that he is hungry and has no soap, I would have to conceal the soap and a few noodles and sneak them to him. Sharing is criminalized in prison also.

I am fortunate to have you and others send money so I don't have to sacrifice my self-respect and dignity slaving for the prison system, or forced to circumvent, manipulate, and deceive to satisfy my needs.

Thank you,
Lacino

Mom & Dad,

I cannot continue to convey to you that I am not trying, nor have I ever tried since being kidnapped and held hostage in this man-made hell hole, to be good. Why don't you try telling me to be intelligent, be ready for whatever comes next, be more human? Anything but keep telling me to be good.

You are going to have to accept that I am no more guilty of my mom's death than you two are. I will not pretend that police and prosecutors did not manufacture this case from whole cloth, because they did. They lied about me because I would not lie about people I did not know. For that lie there is a high price to pay.

I'm not referring to civil suits or anything remotely monetary. That is a very small stage the exonerated play on. Those rewards are fleeting. Old Testament. They are going to pay the price of bitter suffering that I have paid the past seventeen years of my caged life. God is my witness, they are going to pay in full.

There is no crime I could ever commit in pursuit of my freedom as great as the crime committed by those who deny my freedom. No crime whatsoever. When I leave, however I leave, those who deny my freedom will know in unambiguous terms that I am dissatisfied. They will know that I understand each day cataloged and reduced to memory was a day I could not get back. Therefore, I did everything I could that day, today, to correct those that created this dull reality.

That's right, the state of Michigan, county of Wayne, city of Detroit made me an outlaw via false reports and serial witnesses. How is it possible for one person to appear in court every few weeks with tales of another confession? What a remarkable talent. Serial witness Oliver Cowan was an opportunist, a product of the prison environment, which compels men of weak character to curry favor at the expense of others. Well, not me.

The roots of my discontent go much deeper than any particular prison policy or the reaction of administrators. They are to be found in the fact alluded to above: a fifty-two- to eighty-year sentence because I wouldn't testify against men I knew only through street lore and rumor.

To be patient, as you suggest, requires belief that there is something magical about the passing of time. That there is a future waiting. A belief that change happens independent of effort. Well, there isn't, there may not be, and they don't.

Your son,
Lacino Darnell H.

Dear Dr. Fardan,

That is the quickest I have ever written and received a letter back from you. I thought our letters had crossed in the mail until I got into the body of the letter.

You don't even have to ask if I'm coming to Maryland, if I will speak to your classes, or if I will make happen whatever you request of me. I have no idea what the situation would be like today if you hadn't believed in me before I fully believed in myself. Thank you so very much.

Things are status quo here—unworthy of our magnanimous capacity to observe, reflect, and come again. As far as what you wrote about the murder penalty—I was shocked to learn that a man I briefly corresponded with in the late 1990s is still being held on Ohio's death row, nearly twenty years later, in violation of his human and civil rights.

Keith Lamar (a.k.a. Bomani Shakur) was placed on death row following the 1993 prison uprising that occurred at the Southern Ohio Correctional Facility in Lucasville, Ohio. He was placed in solitary confinement, where he has been for the past twenty years and, since 1998, been housed at the Ohio State Penitentiary (supermax) in Youngstown.

According to the state of Ohio, Bomani was the ringleader of a group of inmates dubbed the "Death Squad," who were allegedly responsible for the death of five suspected informants killed during the uprising. However, these claims only came after Bomani refused to become an informant himself and encouraged others not to join sides with the state. If he would have become an informant, he would not be on death row.

Bomani's death sentence is nearing its most critical stage. He has filed his final appeal and request for a hearing before the US Court of Appeals for the Sixth Circuit of Cincinnati, Ohio. If he is not successful, an execution date could be set soon. How isn't this murder? When someone is told to testify for us or be charged with the death penalty, how is that any different from someone putting a gun to someone's head and saying, "Give me your money or die"?

Bomani has written his story in a compelling account entitled *Condemned*. It is available online at Amazon. In it Bomani presents evidence that proves his innocence with actual statements the state willfully withheld. This deprived him of a fair trial, among other things. Since the state was seeking the death penalty, shouldn't everything be put before the jury to make certain they don't get it wrong?

In some very powerful and penetrating prose, Bomani recounts in graphic detail the horror that followed his refusal to become an informant. Painstakingly he paints a clear picture of a justice system that has two conflicting faces: one for rich and one for poor defendants like him. Of course I know all about that. Bomani's story is about justice. A story about what happens when you are poor in a country where justice itself is a commodity that is reserved for those who can purchase it. Bomani did not have money, but like a lot of poor defendants, he could have purchased no prosecution if he would have said what the prosecution wanted him to say.

That is something I think gets overlooked about allowing the prosecution to purchase testimony. When the prosecution decides not to press charges or to reduce charges, it's only if the person being rewarded says what they want them to say. The criteria for receiving consideration is not telling the truth but telling the story that makes the prosecutor's case.

Read his book. Help spread the word. Join the fight to keep Bomani alive. I wonder how he remains so strong. Unquestionably the rounds and rounds of appeals compound the mental pain and suffering of a death row prisoner. Bomani has been forced to live for decades under the psychological torment of a death sentence and in punitive conditions of confinement. I'm going to write Bomani right after this. But there has to be more we can do. The government is killing people not in a so-called immediate danger situation but after years and years of planning, down to the minutest detail. Isn't this the very definition of premeditated murder? I just don't get it how what's illegal for individuals is somehow legal for the state.

I will address the other questions you asked this weekend, after I read the essays you mailed. Take care of yourself.

L. D. Hamilton

Billy,*

You both disappointed and angered me today. I am in a special bind. To get out of trouble, as you insist should be my top priority—which isn't a priority at all—I must show acceptance of the place accorded me, and the place accorded me is to support the occupational role of those who force this bargain. A self-alienating moral servitude, which accounts for why most of the guys forced to be here with me appear to be mental patients: bipolar, paranoid-schizophrenic, delusional disorder, indecisive, apathetic, somatic-type, jealous-type, cowardice, and it continues. That will never be me—one of the broken men.

You should not underestimate the situation here. You are dealing with it too—we all are. There has been no linear progress, not for us as a people. There has been steady subordination of Blacks in one way or another. It only gets worse and costs more when one makes it to a place like this. If examined closely you will see the pattern—cyclical progress and cyclical regression. It pains me that at your advanced age, you're still at step one. I am back in maximum security.

The hearing they gave me was perfunctory. The people who write the policies governing this place are mentally suffering too, or extremely bored. Why would they write so many policies they never intended to follow? That was not a hearing the department gave me. The disposition was decided when officials in Lansing called the prison and told them to segregate me. The hearing officer suppressed evidence, distorted testimony, and constantly interrupted when I spoke. This is not legitimate, and I am not wrong. I would like it if you spoke to me less about trouble-free behavior and more about being effective. You know there are men who have been here only a fraction of the two-and-half decades I have been here who have already prostrated, already given up, given in. Sometimes I wonder, have you? Given up, given in?

---

* Lacino's nickname for his father.

Look at your reaction today when I told you I wear all this sending me back and forth to maximum security as a badge of honor. You think I'm crazy. I heard it in your voice. "Why would you take the more difficult path?" Because I am built different. I have spent the time in here rebuilding, to win.

Perhaps you will understand better when I'm home and you can see for yourself what I have made of myself. But until then do not ask me to stay out of trouble. Prison is trouble, and there just are no two ways about it. Even if you do not understand, encourage me to stay sane, effective, or in the fight.

Lacino Darnell

Dear Shirley & Bob,*

Wishing you a good morning …

When you receive this letter, it may not be morning, and of course several days will have gone by since it was written. Since my major means of communication is a three- or four-day process at best, you never really know how I am doing at any particular moment. You only know how I was feeling or what I was thinking when I sat down to write. It is not like communicating with others by picking up the phone, posting over the computer, or seeing someone live and in the flesh.

The mood and what's happening here can go from bad to worse very quickly. For example, it is six o'clock in the morning and first-shift guards are marching into the housing block right now. They often bring their problems from home to work with them. So as early as 6:01 they can begin exercising their awareness that prisoners make good punching bags. At the same time, prisoners are waking up throughout the housing block from a night of tossing and turning, crying into pillows, reflecting on just how far out of the social order we have fallen and how miserable our lives are. This influences prisoners to exercise the same awareness as guards: punching on others relieves stress. It's sad.

Early in the morning, each morning, a goal for me, like that of a boxer, is to dodge punches and not get hit—I mean that both figuratively and literally. This is one of the many reasons why I hate prison. Every morning I must wake up bobbing, weaving, and running from other people's problems. I suppose that is one of the ways I differ from a punching bag—I don't have to stand there and take it. But the fact that prisoners are even thought of as punching bags means we have taken on somewhat the same characteristics as inanimate objects. Something, not someone, to be acted upon. A frightening position to be in.

Given the psychological characteristics of the human organism, it is obvious that certain adjustments in thinking processes are required to

---

* Parents of Professor Shari, who also became pen pals with Lacino.

make use of people as stress relievers, to do to other human beings what no human being wants done to them. It does not inspire us to expose ourselves to others, to encounter the differences of others' humanness so as to inform and enrich our own. Not when keeping one's guard up at all times appears to be the most prudent thing one can do. But no one can meet their needs, whether they be physical, mental, emotional, or social, always playing defense. Development in those critical areas will likely be stunted. This is fitting for understanding the nature of oppression.

Oppression means social structures and human relations that obstruct fulfillment of needs and, consequently, interfere with individual and social development. Oppression involves domination and exploitation of individuals, communities, and classes, usually initiated by coercive force, followed by socialization and ideological indoctrination. Over time this is internalized by both victim and victimizer, eventually turning the victim into the victimizer.

This is probably a subject I should save for another letter because I really want you to understand that when a victim becomes the victimizer, their actions usually are not directed against the sources, agents, and beneficiaries of the initial victimizing actions. They are displaced onto other victims, which is why there are so many violent feelings, attitudes, relations, and interactions among prisoners. Prisoners use other prisoners as punching bags because administrators and guards have set the tone and built the culture where it is acceptable.

I have not lost my faith in people, however. I will never do that. Bad situations tend to influence bad interactions. And prison definitely qualifies as a bad situation. It is bad for guards and prisoners alike. And it is bad for society as a whole. Eighty percent of people in prison will return to society one day. And when we do, we will bring with us the ideas and habits fostered by the prison.

I am going to read some before breakfast is dropped off, so I am going to bring this to a close. I don't think I got around to the reason I actually sat down to write: to tell you hi and that I was thinking of you. I am certain that by the time this letter arrives, I will still be thinking about you. Looking forward to the day (let's hope soon) that I will be no further from you than a phone call, post, drive, or plane ride away.

Sincerely yours,
Lacino

Dear Helen,[*]

Over the past six months, you have consistently criticized my writings as being anger based. You say the criticism isn't that they contain anger, that you understand the situation here, the overall experience that is, but you feel I do not expound sufficiently enough on the source of my anger and I leave the reader guessing. That my habit is to skip over the basics by mentioning a few of them in a phrase, rather than elaborating for at least a sentence or two about each one. Am I stating your position correctly?

I appreciate you taking the time to critique my essays. It lets me know you are trying to understand what it is I am trying to get across. I have not responded until now simply because I assumed that the more I shared, the more you would get it. Perhaps understand that my anger has been inherited over generations. To show you I value your criticism, I will do my best to address it at length in this correspondence.

I agree with you, not the "angry Black man stereotype," but that I have taken the basics for granted and started somewhere in the middle. I took it for granted that the reader could fill in some of the blanks and did not require an in-depth introduction to how fucked up life is here in prison. I thought that was one thing that everyone understood since no one wants to be behind all these locked doors, high walls, barbed wires, and other barriers to special intercourse. Obviously I was wrong and apologize for taking that for granted. As a rule, going forward, I will take nothing for granted, not even that readers should know that being cut off from the wider society for over two decades, living in an enclosed, formally administered round of life would provoke anger. The dilemma I face now, however, is exactly where to begin.

I am thinking I should go back further than the misconduct guards issued me last week for "aggressive facial gestures," because while that definitely angered me, it is not the source. I was angry long before the

---

[*] A volunteer with the National Coalition to Abolish the Death Penalty who worked on Lacino's case.

people who hold me here gave freedom of expression an entirely new meaning, before I learned how big of a step forward it would be to smile and actually have it reflect how I felt and my prospects for the future.

I am thinking I should go much further back than my transfer last year from an "honor prison" to where I am currently imprisoned: Chippewa Correctional Facility, Michigan's most punitive prison, transferred for receiving literature that calls into question the legitimacy of the prison as a means of administering justice. Literature that explains how prisons do not address structural conditions or arrangements that lead to people harming others.

I am thinking I should go back farther than my arrest, too. Who would not be angry if they were arrested for the death of a family member when they had nothing to do with it? Framed by a detective that after investigating a crime and figuring out the basic facts of a case would then write them out and coach professional jailhouse witnesses to repeat those facts in court and say they were obtained from a confession. Who would not be angry when there is proof of this and the courts refuse to overturn a conviction they know is wrong?

None of those experiences, that would anger anyone, are sufficient for understanding why you correctly sense anger in my writings. If I want readers to really understand, I should begin with what happened in the neighborhood prior to my being kidnapped and held hostage all these years. Yes, that is how I see things. Police showed up at my house with guns drawn, tackled me when I was just standing there with friends enjoying a beautiful summer's afternoon, handcuffed and threw me in the back of a van, and the rest is, as they say, history. Kidnapped. Hostage twenty-three years and running.

I am from the east side of Detroit, Michigan, the 7 Mile/Hoover area but came of age in the infamous Cass Corridor, a known drug den, vice district. A section of the city where discrimination has remained prevalent despite the advances in civil rights made during the Coleman A. Young administration (1974–1994)—Detroit's first Black mayor—where political decisions and social policies led to severe disinvestment and persistent, rigid segregation; where the automotive industry that supported a middle-class urban population migrated away, contracted, and all but collapsed; and where the impact of military-style policing and punitive criminal justice policies were concentrated.

As I sit here and write, I am not all that certain that if the reader understood the economic and social forces that affected my upbringing, and the consequences of those forces, they would be sufficient to understand why anger bleeds through my writings, as you phrase it. Perhaps I have to go even farther back and explain how the forces that affected my upbringing were passed on from my parents to me? Perhaps it is crucial to begin from a multigenerational perspective? I have given this quite a bit of thought, and there is no clear marker indicating how far back I must go to find the source. But it seems logical to consider not only the environment that helped shape me but consider my family's history, too. Does this make sense?

If growing up in a poor and violent neighborhood altered my schooling opportunities, affected who served as my role models, exposed me to pollutants in the air, toxins in the spaces I played, induced extremely high levels of stress, limited my economic opportunities, then it is logical, even reasonable to assume that if my parents were raised in similarly oppressed neighborhoods, witnessed the same violence, and also had few employment opportunities, the impact would be more pronounced for me, reinforced by the consistency of oppression experienced over generations.

The more thought I give to sources, the more impossible I find it for readers to understand anything about me without looking at the history of my immediate family. The effect of being brought up in a severely traumatized family accumulates over generations. For example, my father's imprisonment the first fifteen years of my life, the increased distance his addiction to crack cocaine placed between us, his illiteracy, poor example, crippling advice. His mother's murder the same year of my birth. The hurt and pain he carries with him to this day because my great-grandmother sent him to foster care and took in his other brothers and sisters.

My mother giving birth to me when she was fourteen. The state taking custody of me for the next three and half years. My mother "getting me back" as if I was lost then found just for her to abandon me at a bake sale six months later. Not seeing my mother again until I was eighteen. Her nearly forty-year addiction to drugs and alcohol stemming from the abuse she suffered at the hands of her father. Her father's connection to her mother's death.

The consequences of drowning in abuse and addiction over multiple generations are much more severe than the consequences of personal crises at a single point in time, or even in a single generation. In short, the sources of my anger must be thought of as a continuation of anger that has developed over at least the last eighty years. To put it differently, in the same way that genetic background and financial wealth are passed down from parent to child, the anger you sense in my essays has been inherited. I do not mean I grew up in the same emotional and psychological space as my parents and their parents, but rather I grew up and remain in the same type of social and political crisis. No matter how articulately some people deny it, cumulative experiences provide clues as to how we view and value ourselves.

When my daily experiences conveyed that almost nowhere in society was I respected or granted the ordinary dignity and courtesy accorded to others, as a matter of course, I began to doubt my worth. This doubt became the seed of a pernicious anger. An anger that grew when I learned that the courts did not work for me or thousands of people like me. An anger that actually grew more intense after I was imprisoned and began to self-educate. I know it would seem just the opposite, that education would be liberating and bring me inner peace, but what about outer peace? The more I learned about the American social structure and how it works, the more cheated I felt. I thought people just did not know how pitifully we lived in the Cass Corridor—not true. People who were in positions to do something about how we lived just turned a blind eye. The more I realized that public schools and social services exasperated experiences that were going to be difficult to emerge from with the best resources and assistance.

I don't know if I can elaborate like this every time anger may be picked up on from one of my essays. Should I have to? For some reason this brings to mind the story of the dog and the nation. Are you familiar?

A guy was headed to work early one morning and saw two big flyers posted side by side on a fence outside a public park. One of them had a picture of a small white dog with the words LOST written above it. The other one had a strangely shaped map with the words LOST NATION written above in red. What surprised the man was the huge number of people packed around the picture of the beautiful white dog, while the flyer for the missing nation sign remained neglected, not drawing the attention of a single person.

Do you think people that do not care would care?

Lacino Darnell H.

Dear Andrea,*

I was the first of my mother's, Brenda Hamilton's, six children, born November 11, 1974. Ruthie, my mother's older and only sister, once said I was born in a DSS bathroom. I doubt the validity of that. My aunt Ruthie habitually makes things up. My mother was fourteen when she gave birth to me and she was a ward of the state of Michigan. I am a legacy baby—at birth I was taken into state custody, became a ward of the state, too. My father, Lacino Plummer, was eighteen, incarcerated at the Michigan Reformatory in Ionia, Michigan. My father was serving the first of four prison sentences. He would spend over two decades in and out of prison. Another legacy marker. Much of my young life, I bounced from foster placement to foster placement.

Foster placement was a lot like prison. First, there were areas that were off-limits or out of bounds. Being there was actively prohibited, unless, for example, one was with an authorized staff or performing a service role. Second, there were surveillance areas ruled less by the physical presence of staff and more by physical barriers, technology, and the understanding of the meaning of my position in foster placement. Finally, there was the most valued area constantly encroached on by the first two, my heart and mind. Areas in which the ordinary levels of surveillance and restrictions were markedly reduced, where I could engage in a range of taboo activities with some degree of independence. It was the only place I was free to be myself.

As far as my formal education is concerned, I had a lot of starts and stops. Bouncing from foster placement to foster placement there was a lot of abrupt moving, waiting on school records to follow, lost school records, "makes no sense to enroll you in school since you will not be here long." However, I was delivered from this humiliation and lack of education shortly after my eleventh birthday when I ran away from one of the foster

---

* A professor in Alaska who became a pen pal of Lacino's.

homes and began living on the streets of Detroit. Hungry, afraid, aware of how small and weak I was, I learned quickly to raise my voice and use weapons. I learned that family isn't always determined by blood but by who has your back and whose back you have. I learned a lot of variations of doing bad, and that a lot of people were doing bad. I learned that Reagan was a name you did not say unless it was preceded by "that motherfuckah." I learned on the streets what would have brought me huge rewards on Wall Street. That taking risk, running up on difficulty, and entertaining the forbidden is proof of a "get up, get out, and get something" sort of character—highly valued and respected qualities.

From ages eleven to fourteen, I lived in what were called "spots" in Detroit. To the rest of the country, they were known as crack houses. I lived there and spent most of the day handing people who knocked on the back door or side window pieces of crack cocaine through a small cutout in exchange for balled-up money—sometimes change—but my eighteen-year-old boss, Howard Johnson, did not like me accepting change. Howard Johnson was to me a big brother, a mentor, a father figure.

Howard Johnson (he was always addressed by his first and last name) spent a lot of time teaching me about the ways of the world, how to navigate it, and something he loved to say, "how to get this money." Howard Johnson is what was called a street legend, revered for being a millionaire four or five times over before his eighteenth birthday. In the "mother-fuckah-ing" Reagan era, that was no small feat. I hung on to his every word as if it were chapter and verse.

Howard Johnson taught me that who I know and who I associate and am seen with says a lot about me, so I should be careful about who I befriend. It said a lot about me that I was his right-hand man. Being in the company of Howard Johnson was like being in the company of a rock star or a head of state. He was phenomenal.

At age fourteen, my days of being a runaway came to an end. A routine traffic stop resulted in my arrest and being sent to training school in Adrian, Michigan. Living on my own since I was eleven, I never reconciled with there being so many rules, having no say in the planning of my day, or having to ask for permission to do things like speak or use the bathroom. From the moment I got there I was determined to escape back to where my voice was loud and my decisions were my own. Before I did, the most unlikely thing happened: a handsome man in a tan suit, brown wing-tipped Stacey Adams, brown Kangol golf cap, and a large smile came walking from the administration building and stopped right in front of me. "You are Lacino. If you were a pebble on the beach, I would know you." It was my father.

My father had been released from San Quentin Prison in California two years earlier. He explained to me how he had been searching for me since his release and had just learned of my whereabouts the night before. We instantly connected. He kept trying to explain his absence, but it wasn't necessary. I was no longer the only Lacino Darnell I knew. Most of all, we were going to be a family, father and son, big Lacino and Little Lacino (I took to the name immediately) versus everyone else. This brought me a better feeling than being Howard Johnson's right-hand man. I didn't think there could be a better feeling than that. Still, I had escape on my mind.

The escape was poorly planned but nonetheless successful. During a weekly scheduled horseback event where my group assisted disabled children riding horses, me and a few members of the group asked for permission to go to the bathroom that was outside the barn where the event was held, and ran. We ran for about an hour through the woods, finally finding a road and a pay phone. I promised one of the guys whose mother came to give him a ride back to Inkster, Michigan, that if she drove me to Detroit I would give her five hundred dollars. She was skeptical that I had the money to give her, but after speaking with Howard Johnson, who promised to give her twice that much, she let me in the car.

About a month later, I was arrested for curfew violations. Instead of sending me back to the training school in Adrian, I was sent to St. Jude's Home for Boys, five minutes from Howard Johnson's mother's house. St.

Jude's was a halfway house for teenagers. Basically I just slept there. During the day I attended classes at Demby High School, four blocks away. During the afternoons and evenings, I hung out at Howard Johnson's mother's house. He would come by from time to time and let me know that whenever I wanted to come back to work for him, I could. But I was determined to keep going to school and when school was out to go live with my father and be a family, but that did not happen.

I had no idea that my father was addicted to crack. Perhaps because I only saw him on weekends it was easy for him to hide his addiction, but after he stole $20,000 from a drug dealer who lived in his apartment building, his secret came out. I really thought we were going to be a family and that I would never sell crack again—that just wasn't to be if I wanted to prevent my father from being killed.

I had to beg the guy to let me pay him back and seek no retribution from my father. Sending a message to others who might try the same seemed to mean more to him than the money. I agreed to give him an extra $10,000. I got the money from Howard Johnson by driving a moving van from Las Vegas to Detroit. There were secret compartments built into the van where drugs were hidden. I never told my father exactly how I got the money, but he knew it wasn't legal. I don't think he cared much; he was just happy to come out of hiding.

I love my father, but I also resented him. I may have even hated him. Our plans of being a family went up in smoke, literally. My father and I went from building a relationship to no relationship at all, so I returned to selling drugs for Howard Johnson to support myself. It was a dark time and I went to a dark place. And I may have remained there had I not been arrested and subsequently convicted for the shooting death of my foster mother, Willa Bee Bias.

A point I want to note here is the curious difficulty I have in feeling innocent despite having no knowledge or participation in that crime. Everything about the way I was living created an atmosphere where something like that was likely to happen. I did not realize back then, but when drugs are introduced to a community, it is just a matter of time before the community and the people in it deteriorate into chaos. Wherever there are drugs, there is also dishonesty, theft, and violence of all kinds—emotional as well as physical. My actions had consequences that far exceeded the personal harm it brought to people addicted to the drugs I sold. I wish I had understood this back then.

I am going to fast-forward to being convicted of my mother's death and sentenced to prison for fifty-two to eighty years. It took me years to find a secret police memorandum detailing how the prosecution's star and only witness, a jailhouse informant, was told exactly what to say by detectives when he took the stand. He was a professional witness who testified in numerous murder cases where detectives told him exactly what to say.

Prison? The monotony, idle time, loneliness, constant will-breaking tactics employed by prison officials, and the possibility of violent attack that could be brought on at any time for any disrespect, real or imagined, were all driving me insane. I did a lot of self-medicating with marijuana and prison-made liquor, read law books I did not understand, and rebelled in very desperate ways. I was in prison a little over a year before being accused of a plan to assault the warden. I spent four years in solitary confinement for that.

I would be remiss if I did not tell you about Adika Mensah and the role he played in my life during this time. Adika, my first direct contact with a prisoner intellectual, possessed a definite spirit of independence and an awareness of the prisoner population as a group with potential strength to manifest itself in many ways. He was one of the Malcolm X, Eldridge Cleaver, Alprentice "Bunchy" Carter strain. He impressed on me that knowledge is power. And that it was going to take a power superior to that which put me in prison to get me out. I committed myself to becoming very knowledgeable. So with a great deal of effort and determination, seriousness and discipline, I began to educate myself.

I read constantly. I started out reading African and Black history because those were the books in Adika's personal library. There was a lot of emphasis placed on economics and politics, acquiring and using power. I began to better understand systems, and that if systems were understood, I could figure out how to navigate them.

It did not happen all at once, but slowly, over time I began to acquire an intellectual life—a love for small details and context, history, multiple sides of a single story, notions of justice and dignity, certain central values, and knowing for the sake of just knowing. It seems only natural that I developed a desire to write. It was the only way I could get the transformation taking place inside my head and heart into the real world. I had a real desire to connect with other people. Writing presented me with opportunities to do that.

This is the quick version, but I hope it answers some of your questions.

Lacino

Carl,

I think you have the concept of oppression too narrowly defined, and that's problematic.

Oppression is more than and distinct from just being beat up by the police or given a court-appointed lawyer who performs like their degree is in flipping burgers—not that I have anything against people who grind it out in front of a fryer, just making a point. Oppression is an interlocking system that involves domination and control of social ideology, social institutions, and resources of the society. This vertical and horizontal domination and control provides the base for which white supremacist ideology defines and determines what is allegedly normal, real, correct, and the like.

Antonio Gramsci, whose book *Selections from the Prison Notebook* that I am reading right now, describes this as hegemony.[2] He writes that hegemony controls the way ideas become common sense. Like it is common sense to incarcerate someone if they are responsible for fracturing, breaking, or harming property or another person, right? Wrong. There is nothing common sense about an institution that has about a three-hundred-year history. But it's very much common sense to most people, even people who recognize the harm caused by caging people for part or all of their lives, so common sense that most people cannot imagine a world without prisons.

When beliefs, policies, and practices are widespread and pervasive, people don't have to be cold and calculating, and that isn't to imply that people aren't. But it is difficult for a lot of people to step outside of the system to see it from a different perspective, to see the system for what it really is—a socially constructed ideology that perpetuates a particular set of hierarchical relationships among different groups. As bad as some family and friends want me home, they aren't thinking about abolishing the prison system. I sound crazy to them when I bring this up. They just hope one of these innocence projects gets on board and gets me out.

I will give you a simple way to test what I am saying. Ask people at random to tell you the first thing that comes to their mind when you say the word "crime." Just ask them the first thing they think of. More likely than not, they are going to answer with something related to poor people and/or people of color. They aren't going to answer by talking about all the deception and graft taking place on Wall Street, the new round of sanctions just slapped on Iran, the disproportionate benefits of Trump's tax cuts, wage suppression, wars of choice, none of the atrocious actions that are elite sponsored. Instead their minds are going to automatically focus on something taking place in the hood, something that a black or brown face can be attached to. Unless they've been in dialogue with one like Kwasi or Yusef. And sometimes that's not enough.

White supremacy isn't some cowardly actions of some white guy with a confederate flag tied to the back of his truck. Well, it could be that. But in the larger sense, it's the power to misrepresent, discount, erase, or appropriate what we produce. It's culture defined by standards and norms that benefit whites. It's the association of crime with poor people and people of color. It's all sorts of built-in explanations for why so many of us show up on prison count sheets and assumptions about the naturalness and the inevitability of things as they are. And the more natural things appear, the more difficult it will be for more people to identify, analyze, and challenge them.

You can't just focus on the spectacular episodes of oppression, the things that make the news and think that when people grab a placard and take to the street that oppression is being challenged. Oppression is like water to fish. It's everywhere. Primordial to the culture. And we are going to have to come out of it. Stop thinking we can't live outside of it. And that's the long and short of it.

Lacino

Dear Comrade,

I appreciate your letters a lot. You always present me with something insightful, even when I do not agree with you, like now. Police, courts, and prisons do not eliminate harmful interactions. First, harmful interactions do not begin or end with gang banging, selling drugs, killing members of our community, or any of the other media-grabbing actions that you list. Those are not the only actions that harm the community.

The problem with this perspective is that it narrowly restricts the discussion of who harms the community to low-hanging fruit. The categories of who harm our communities are clearly broader than your list and relate to a range of people, including bankers, land developers, politicians, corporate boards/shareholders, and judges that legitimize and protect the often disastrous outcomes of their growth projections.

The unnecessary restriction you place on who we should focus on eliminating from the community means that one of the thorniest issues community members must tackle is avoided: how to consider the relationships between rebellion as a remedy for gross violations of human rights when the offender is the state, corporations, and their agents.

Second, strong communities eliminate crime, not police and prisons. I will primarily focus my response here since you spilled most of your ink arguing the opposite.

I agree with you. "Shit has gotten so bad" that almost any member of the community can become a victim. As a result community members that just want to feel safe and protected have themselves called for increased policing and more and longer prison sentences. But you know, police only come, if they come, after "the shit has went down." To be an intellectual, I love your colorful use of the English language. Shit it is.

One of the biggest obstacles in attempting to better understand how to eliminate harmful behavior in the community is that we are trying to do so through statistics. Statistics that obscure more than clarify the problem. Not just because of their unreliability in terms of sources, definitions, and the extent to which their meaning is slanted by interests other than solving our problems, but also because statistics only hint at the real problem—a lack of community and exercising the power of community.

One of the issues that receives attention when discussing how to make the community safer is the insufficiency of resources at the disposal of the community. While others equate businesses, jobs, and money with community resources, I don't. Our communities can definitely use more of them, but when I say insufficiency of resources, I am referring to the mechanisms that make communities go: control of major institutions like banks and utilities and decision-making power that cannot be approved or vetoed by city hall.

More jobs and higher incomes will not stop the drug dealing and robberies. If we are not the ones bringing jobs and higher incomes into the community, we cannot stop them from leaving. But when we control banks, we can finance our own moneymaking opportunities. When we control utilities, we can make them nonnegotiable human rights. And when we do not have to plead with, pray to, or threaten to burn down city hall—to get what belongs to us anyway like it is some kind of special gift—we can make community policy. Regardless of how great the need is, city hall only gives it to us when it will do the most good for city hall.

Another issue that receives a fair share of criticism is one that suggests if we fix it, our communities will be safer: how inadequate the public school system is now. However, the lens in which the criticism is presented is cloudy. I am not going to enumerate the usual criticisms. What I will do is present a lens from which we can actually view the education crisis: from the earliest age, most students are aware that what they are being taught is not designed to identify or solve their most basic problems. When they react with hostility and aggression toward teachers and the education process, it is because their dignity and potential as human beings are being ignored and suppressed.

They are aware they are being prepared for future societal irrelevance. Up-to-date books and computers in each classroom will not prevent actions that make the community unsafe. Education has to be based on the primary cause of social problems—powerlessness. The cure for powerlessness is power. The criteria for solving America's problem of crime is, in fact, very simple (even though the execution of such an education would be enormously difficult and complex). Power must be redistributed; that redistribution will then permit real decision-making and not a bunch of choices that are peripheral in nature.

Another issue that receives quite a bit of attention and criticism is community leadership, which there is never a shortage of. There are community leaders of one kind or another to overflow stadiums. The problem is not that there is an absence of community leadership or that it is of an inferior quality. The problem is that community leaders lack power to make change happen by its own will and its own action. Community leadership does not in itself provide the financial or the organizational stability for long-range conflict because it is too dependent on resources that lie beyond the boundaries of the community.

Community leadership often subjects itself to the control of others it believes holds primary power. It is prepared to make petty concessions to give the appearance of getting things done. But no one is fooled. What they are getting done is like shaving two grams of a pound—so small no one notices what has been done in their day-to-day lives.

Unable to compete successfully for power or patronage, community leaders tend to compete among themselves for the available crumbs from foundations or from "one of the ones who made it out" in order to say they are "doing something." This in turn makes them more susceptible and vulnerable to manipulation and being co-opted. As a consequence, the community often has little or no faith in community leadership. Even the very committed leaders.

What we are accustomed to thinking of as making the community unsafe are actually the straightforward manifestations of the dynamics of a lack of power. A community that is powerless is not really a community. It is a neighborhood, places where people live but do not control the institutions that impact their lives. So when I say strong communities eliminate crime, that means the people who live in the neighborhood possess the requisite economic and political power to provide for their own internal needs.

What we need to be safe and protected is a very fundamental change in direction. We should continue a lot of private, small-scale things that people are already doing (e.g., develop block clubs, internal economies, skill banks, mentorship programs, neighborhood cleanups, and educational models centered on developing independent power sources). But they all have to be aimed toward acquiring, using, and maintaining power, for which there are no ready-made models to follow. We have to begin where there is consensus, using what we got until we get what we need.

I am with you 100 percent. But institutions based on coercion and force cannot eliminate problems that are the result of coercion and force. If you think about it, if that were true, no place on earth should be safer than America. The world's top cop and jailer.

Rebuild to win,
Lacino

"Visionary feminists have always understood the necessity of converting men. We know all the women in the world could become feminist but if men remain sexist our lives would still be diminished. Gender warfare would still be a norm."

—bell hooks[3]

Dear Shirley & Bob,

A request has come across my desk to write a short essay on the unprecedented challenges incarceration poses to women. I am so open and up to this. The challenges confronting women behind bars does not receive attention commensurate to the crisis.

It is difficult to imagine more compelling evidence that incarceration has damaged the American social structure than the near 1000 per 100,000 male incarceration rate. The number of men divided from their family and community has sent both into a tailspin headed downward into dysfunction. However, the incarceration rate of women has increased faster than that of men since 1977. There are more than a half million women incarcerated around the world, with more than one-third caged here. Do you follow? America is 5 percent of the world's population and 35 percent of the world's incarcerated women are in American prisons. Make that make sense.

I am anxious to contribute to bring awareness, and hopefully resources to stop this madness. American incarcerated women are disproportionately racial and ethnic minorities. Black women are incarcerated at a rate almost three times higher than that of white women. Latino women incarceration rates fall between that of Black and white women. Migrant women from Central and South America are being incarcerated at rates so alarming, liberation forces should do their thing.

Laws such as the 1986 Immigration Reform and Control Act (IRCA) and the Illegal Immigration Reform and Immigrant Responsibility Act (IIRAIRA) have served to criminalize migrant women. I just don't see how our country can criminalize people who are going to such extremes to make a better life. Crime policies disguised as immigration reform. The IRCA extended the war on drugs to the border. The IIRAIRA reclassified some minor offenses as aggravated felonies. These laws have helped sweep migrant women into the war on drugs and resulted in the dividing of migrant women from their children. In some cases women have been deported after serving their sentence, and their children were put in foster care. Where is the justice in that?

Looking beyond racial and ethnic make-up, some studies suggest that the percentage of incarcerated women who experience physical, psychological, and/or sexual violence prior to incarceration is higher than 75 percent.[4] That is higher than the number of nonincarcerated women who report violence. Equally high is the percentage of incarcerated women who are mothers of children under eighteen years of age. Even higher is the number that have been diagnosed with mental health issues or who report that they regularly used drugs. Many of the women behind bars have serious physical health problems including hepatitis, diabetes, and HIV/AIDS infections.

I plan to include this information in order to draw a portrait of the class and needs of the women that are being locked up. The media tends to show the same image of women behind bars, and it is not a flattering one. Media images have framed incarcerated women as violent and out of control. Women's incarceration rate is not the result of an increase in violence. Only about one-third of women were sentenced for violent crimes. A lot of times this is the result of fending off male attackers. Drug offenses are actually the largest source of growth. About one-third of women compared to one-fifth of men serve time for drug offenses.

Mandatory minimum sentences and sentencing guidelines emerged largely from the war on drugs in the 1980s. These measures required judges to hand down lengthy sentences based on the amount of the drug without taking into consideration extenuating circumstances: prior records, context of the offense, abuse that could have led to addiction, the low-level role that women usually play in drug offenses. It is well known in legal circles that even though women generally play small roles in drug offenses, they are more likely to be arrested, convicted, and incarcerated than they were prior to the failed war on drugs. Men who use vulnerable women as drug couriers literally leave women to get caught holding the bag.

Tough sentencing laws eliminated judicial consideration of women's roles as primary caretakers of children. When women are incarcerated, the burden of child care often falls to extended family, including grandparents and distant relatives. When this isn't an option, children are placed in foster care. This demographic makes up about 15 percent of the foster care system.[5]

Under the Adoption and Safe Families Act (ASFA) of 1997, agencies are required to move to "permanency planning"—including termination of parental rights—when children are in foster care for fifteen of the previous twenty-two months. This practice is rather common considering that when women are sentenced to prison, their children are more likely to be placed in foster care than when men (fathers) are sentenced to prison.

The majority of children with incarcerated parents live more than one hundred miles away from their mother's place of confinement. This makes visitation very challenging. It makes intensive mothering all but impossible. Studies show that even when women are incarcerated, if they can maintain emotional and physical connections with their children, they show far fewer behavioral problems and are two times less likely to spend time incarcerated.

A friend of mine, Dr. Lora Bex Lampert, wrote a book I cannot stop telling people about—*Women Doing Life: Gender, Punishment and the Struggle for Identity*. Once they are in prison, women's lives continue to be marred by neglect and abuse. Women are subject to routine searches, harassment, and sexual assault by guards. The Prison Rape Elimination Act (PREA) was passed in 2003. It set the national standards to prevent sexual assault and rape in American prisons. Rape still occurs. Mostly by guards. It should not be overlooked that sexual violence is also emotional and psychological. The wounds and scars, while invisible to the eye, can last a lifetime.

While the system to prevent and confront sexual assault in prison is inadequate, physical and mental health care is even worse. Medical care is substandard in all facilities but more so in women's prisons, considering their needs. Women entering prison have high rates of infectious diseases, respiratory and digestive system issues, genitourinary disorders, and skin and musculoskeletal diseases that often go untreated. Gynecological care is considered a specialty service and therefore only offered after a problem has reached crisis status. The frequency of hysterectomies is criminal.

Pregnant women receive little or no prenatal or postnatal care. The infant mortality rate for mothers in prison is three times higher than for the population at large. Frequently women give birth in shackles and are sent back to the prison a few hours later. This is the definition of cruel and unusual punishment.

My mood has changed since I started this letter. The challenges incarceration poses to women are depressing. I try not to forget that incarceration is gendered. And why wouldn't it be? All of America is gendered. I am going to have to lay down for a while and try to boost my energy level. Sorry.

Feminism is for everybody,
Lacino

Dear Rhonda,

Your letter gave me the opportunity for a real smile. Not one of those "fake it until I make it" smiles, the only type I manage these days. It is difficult to smile through the daily rounds of threats of punishment to induce me to cooperate and penalties when I don't. But your letter—I am smiling right now, ear to ear.

You know just what to say to make me feel decisive. The only person who doesn't ask me to go along to get along. The only person that seems to understand there is something more to my life than avoiding penalties and sanctions. You know, the right to dignity, self-expression, and opportunities for creativity. These clearly acknowledge that I am more than 247310—the number the state of Michigan has branded me with—clearly acknowledges I still have strength to rebel and have not given in to defeat and never will.

I explain to everyone who supports me that after the prison believes who we were prior to incarceration has been shaken by the stripping process, it is largely the "privilege system" that provides a framework for our reorganization. Formal and informal instruction on how to receive a small amount of rewards that shouldn't even be thought of as rewards. Like being left alone and not harassed, something we should be able to expect anyway, but can't. Greatly increasing the psychological stresses of twenty-three hours in cell, one hour out.

The privilege system, and that is the penological name for it, is comprised of three basic elements. First, there are the rules given to us when we arrive and told to memorize because if they are violated, "you will pay." These rules lay out the main requirements of conduct. Chief among them, follow all commands from all staff regardless of what they are. Even if it is a ludicrous command, "follow it and complain later." Yeah, I couldn't make that up. Coded within that get down or lay down mob mentality is, "complain later," which delegitimizes legitimate grievances by referring to them as "complaining." But I will save that for another letter.

Second, a small number of privileges are held out in exchange for obedience, like we are dogs or something. Dogs obey. People work together. These potential gratifications are carved out of activities previously taken for granted, such as a hot cup of coffee instead of having to use tap water or an eight-minute shower instead of a five-minute one. These are the sort of things held out in exchange for "obedience." I challenge anyone to try to smile through that.

The third element of the privilege system is an elaborate system of consequences and punishments. It's insane to think that I am treated like a child. And I greatly dislike using that reference because seldom do we acknowledge that children are treated as if they do not have minds of their own and were put on earth to be bossed around. Children are not treated like coparticipants in discovery and development.

The prison leads with consequences and punishment. Everything from the suspension of all privileges, psychological mistreatment such as ridicule and vicious ribbing, to moderate and sometimes severe corporal punishment. Consequences and punishments come first and lessen only when we pretend the prison is helping us. This is some twisted Hammer Films–type stuff. This brings to mind waterboarding or some other "stress technique," which is what the Bush administration was calling torture, the infliction of pain to bring about a desired behavior. But none of this, at least not at the moment, can stop me from smiling.

I thank you for writing and the kind things you said about my character. You're right, I will not give in to ignorance or mean-spiritedness. There is no victory in that. The victory is in, even after being subjected to unfair and excessive punishment more degrading than that prescribed by law, I haven't decided to get even or take reprisals. With that decision I win. I'm not and never will be what the prison tries so hard to make me out to be.

Smiling,
Lacino

Rhonda,

Whoever you spoke with on the phone "spun you." That's what prisoners call it when we attempt to resolve a problem and staff says anything they think we might want to hear just to get us out of their faces. "Spun" as in talk circles around us. Don't feel like you have failed me, this is a specialized role fulfilled by staff trained in appeasement and deflection.

Seriously, I believe the department trains in this skill. There will always be a need to spin prisoners and members of the wider society because staff actions will never match standards. Plus, all conflicts cannot be threatened away. That is not the most effective way to interact with members of society. Therefore, there will always be a need for staff members that can "spin" effectively.

In many ways it is an act of insanity for us to attempt to resolve conflict in this manner. It is not as if we walk away and figure out at some later time that we have been spent. We are aware at the moment it is happening that everything we are being told is to appease, deflect, and move us along. More than likely there will be a line of prisoners with grievances since staff trained in the art of spinning make themselves accessible to the prisoner population so rarely.

You might think of these spin artists, which is a common way the prisoner population describes these men and women, as prison politicians. Prison staff who provide a personal symbol of the institution to prisoners—as well as to visitors and others connected to us. A symbol on which we may project many different kinds of emotions while staff stand there and nod, agree, and smile, knowing that no action will be taken in our favor.

What also makes this an act of insanity is while these spin artists do not perform the immediate task of violating humane standards, they do not perform the immediate task of handing out consequences and punishments, it is on their orders that consequences and punishments are carried out. You spoke with the warden, right? She is the person that instructed all other prison staff to violate court orders and decrease legal research from six hours per week to one. Yet she told you she will "look into why prisoner Hamilton is not allowed more legal research time." She is the reason.

Staff spin artists give the impression that the guard or staff member most immediately in violation of this or that humane standard, who are likely at the bottom of the staff hierarchy (which is what brings them into immediate contact with prisoners), is the villain. And the spin artist who sits at or near the top is really good. An expression of this appears in actual politicians who occasionally hold town hall meetings and feign disbelief or concern to learn of this or that community problem that originates behind closed-door meetings they either host or attend with other social planners and policy makers. This is the same sort of insanity because we obtain some sense of security from hearing them speak, illusionary as it is, that they will solve our problems.

On a lower level, but just as nefarious, prisoner trustees often spin for the prison. They will spread news of some pending or soon-to-be-implemented abuse as they go about sweeping, serving food trays, or some other menial task. In times past these prisoners were called straw (i.e., stand-in) bosses. While spreading information unfavorable to the prisoner population, information given to them by prison staff, they also spread justifications that were also given to them by prisoner staff. In this way the anger and frustration is leveled at the trust. So do not feel like you failed me, you haven't.

Just know if there is ever reason for you to call on my behalf again, the person on the other end of the phone will say anything to convince you the problem you describe is unknown to them, but nonetheless a priority to be solved—and they will be "spinning" you. In the vernacular, they will be lying. We must devise ways to express our grievances from a position of power. Power is the ability to put our ideas in play and have others adhere to them as if they were their own. Get it?

Thank you for caring and being uniquely you.

Appreciate you. The fault is never yours. It always rests at the feet of those who created the problem in need of being solved in the first place.

Lacino

Takura,

Walking from the administration building back to the tombs (the cell block) after the visit was over, I felt wound up. Super, super tight. Like if I took one more step, even a baby step, I was going to explode in frustration. Why is so much effort required to undo and correct an obvious miscarriage of justice?

It defies all forms of intelligence to think that two or three men could be the star witnesses in dozens of cases, claiming in each to have received unsolicited confessions, at the same precinct, where they lived for months and years when the legal stay is only forty-eight to seventy-two hours. Wayne County prosecutors and judges swore the same oath you and Mary swore.

At that moment all I could do was cry. I didn't care who saw me. I wanted to scream, punch, stomp, drop to my knees, and strike both fists down to the ground. There aren't many options in here to unwind. If I had done anything but cry, I probably would have been gang tackled by guards and dragged off to segregation. Just another instance where what I think and feel has to be suppressed.

I blame a lot of this on the judge-made doctrine of "quality immunity." This doctrine, invented out of whole cloth, immunizes public officials from being held accountable for their actions, even when they commit illegal misconduct. It's not just a protection from accountability but also an entitlement not to stand trial or face the burdens of litigation.

Which means police, prosecutors, and judges are not actually required to pursue what they consider justice (i.e., winning) within the boundaries of any rules. They can withhold evidence, suborn perjury, and even recruit a cadre of professional witnesses and tell them exactly what to testify to, and no one is held accountable.

Qualified immunity is like playing a card game where jokers are wild, and at any time, police, prosecutors, and judges can claim every card they are holding is a joker. What then guarantees a fair trial? What prevents police, prosecutors, and judges from going wild? It definitely isn't the oath they swore to repair and restore relationships back to health. Which is what justice is, repairing what's been damaged, restoring what's been broken. Not a doctrine that lacks any legal basis, vitiates the power of individuals to vindicate their constitutional rights, and contributes to a culture of near-zero accountability for police, prosecutors, judges, and many other public officials.

Another contributing factor to the lack of accountability is the practice of settling lawsuits with taxpayer money rather than challenging protective laws and police unions willing to spend substantial amounts on litigation. Millions of taxpayer dollars are spent, nobody admits wrongdoing, and the wrongdoers remain in place. Weak oversight and no accountability mechanisms can't help but produce situations like mine.

Have you had an opportunity to speak with anyone at the Conviction Integrity Unit or the Free Press writer since the visit? I should take the lead on both of them. There is only so much time you and Mary can commit to being a squeaky wheel, which does happen to receive the oil. If you can get their addresses, phone numbers, and names in the mail to me this week, I would greatly appreciate it.

Part of the reason I am wound up so tight is I've just been sitting here doing nothing. That doesn't take away from the work you and Mary are doing, but no amount of work done by others justifies me doing none. I have and continue to view this as a partnership, requiring coparticipation, cowork.

Thank you for making the long drive to the prison. Seven hours one way? I'm sure you understand why I say I'm in exile. Thank Mary, Cavanagh, Kim, and the others at the office.

Lacino D. Hamilton

Carl,

I am going to just start out by saying that I emphatically disagree with you saying that some people have earned the right to say whatever they want because of their contributions to and during the Civil Rights Movement. That is not only folly but a dangerous policy. What if they come out and say we should just submit to oppression? I am going to assume you would have a problem with them saying that, which means they do not have a right to say whatever they want. And while many have not come out and said we should submit in such direct terms, capitulation after capitulation has screamed just that.

To be truthful, I have been thinking for quite some time that we have to find a respectful way to tell some of these old civil-rights types that we honor their sacrifices but that they are fighting past their prime. Find a respectful way to break it to them that they are not the social justice fighter they once were. It is a difficult conversation to have because when someone once excelled in something and it is basically all they've known, seldom do they know when to call it quits, even when their performance is embarrassing. To use a basketball analogy, it came a time when even the basketball god himself, Michael Jordan, had to retire his Nike Airs.

To aficionados and social justice contemporaries, it's sad to watch anyone who was once at the top of their game continue to compete (for lack of a better word), with a diminished set of skills. That is what we are witnessing. Most (if not all) of the civil rights greats are not anymore. Matter of fact, I am not going to drag this argument out. To return back to the basketball analogy, no matter how great Michael Jordan was, or how he is ranked in the pantheon of professional basketball players, the operative word is "was." He no longer laces up the Nike Airs, and if he did he would be embarrassed.

Being great in contemporary terms really boils down to thoughts, aspirations, hopes, desires, analyses, and critiques of all kinds, being based on sharing tragedies that they no longer share. At least not the brunt of them. They have become as foreign to the tragedies and people they claim to speak for as the ideologues and professional politicians who profess to have all the answers. Some of them are ideologues and professional politicians.

They are older statesmen and stateswomen that we should consult with when appropriate, it would be foolish to dismiss the knowledge many have acquired from battles fought, some won, but it is virtually impossible to accept them as leaders at this day in time. A lot of them only show up when our anger spills over into the streets and they are imploring us to clear out and wait on the finding of some investigation where the perpetrators investigate themselves. They ask us to do something many of them refused to do at one time.

It does not matter if they approve or disapprove of our actions—the fact is we are in the middle of the very tragedies they pontificate about. We cannot indulge in the sterile, wishful thinking of people whose alleged authority to say whatever they want is rooted in what they did sixty years ago rather than with actual contributions right here, right now, today. And I am not saying they cannot speak, surely they can. Only that what they say is subject to the same analyses and criticisms as you, me, or anyone else.

Lacino Darnell Hamilton

Carl,

There is no delicate way to say this, so I will just come out with it, reintroducing higher education into prison with the blessing and support of legislators and prison officials is not going to happen anytime in the foreseeable future. At least not in any substantial way. And no amount of lobbying or "pressure" will change this.

The truth is there is social inequality and social ranking in American life. Some people are in fact considered to be more valuable than others. That being so, it should not be particularly surprising to discover that incarcerated men and women are not valued. We are not valued as members of the larger society, and quite frankly, we are not valued as human beings with minds and the intellectual capacity to do more than follow simple commands.

There are volumes of pseudoscience declaring prisoners possess emotional and psychological handicaps that prevent academic achievement. Therefore, we supposedly not only need a different approach in the education process but a different type of education all together. So instead of offering us intellectually rigorous and stimulating academic courses, we are given "programming" based upon regimentation and blind obedience.

The assumption is that high academic standards will only frustrate us, so the so-called humanitarian thing to do is not to set academic goals for us at all. This is academic atrophy. The wasting away of human potential. The perpetuation of traditional social differences. Face it, there are tens of thousands of college graduates that cannot find employment commensurate with their particular fields of expertise. The chances of people released from prison with college degrees leap-frogging past them is slim to none. Often prisoners are lucky to find menial work, if any work at all. The theory is, more degrees will only saturate the market and make degrees less valuable than they are becoming.

Then you have those that say we are damaged goods and any investment in us is a bad investment, an alibi for maintaining juridically fixed and crystalized estates of division. The fallacy does not mean that policies or practices based on pseudoscience and porous alibis will be demonstrated ineffective. To the contrary, what it does mean is that when someone is treated as if they cannot achieve high academic learning, almost invariably they do not. Not necessarily for lack of aspiration or lack of ability but for disregard and lack of opportunity.

Believe it or not, there are groups in society that do not want us leaving prison with the quality of education that facilitates the type of insights and understanding of our predicament that might inconvenience or challenge those with privilege, wealth, and power. What many people seem to forget is that in the early 1950s and 1960s when Black people were on college and university campuses in large numbers, for the first time in American history, the information and knowledge acquired significantly contributed to rebellion. That's because oppression + education = resistance.

The fear is that when we are released back into society, back into the very conditions that spawned our frustrated and desperate acts of defiance, armed with legitimate critical thinking and analytical skills, they will inevitably lead to organized resistance. Think about it, part of the problem is, most people do not know what's really going on, and far fewer really understand what must be done to put a stop to it. For those that want to keep political and social arrangements status quo, that is a winning formula.

Furthermore, it is not only feared that we will use education to resist oppression when released—prisons have long been an extreme reflection of the American system itself—prison officials are well aware that it is easier to dominate and control an ignorant population than one that is informed. That is another reason why higher education is not coming back to prison in any substantial way. Denying prisoners access to intellectually rigorous and stimulating academic courses is preventive action to break up resistance before it can get started. Preventive action before prisoners can begin to thinking about issues beyond the prison, victims other than themselves, and how it is all connected. This is the same reason inner city schools work the way they do.

Inner city schools are not broken, so we need to stop perpetuating that propaganda. Inner city schools that cause unhappiness, boredom, apathy in learning, and diminished levels of curiosity are working according to plan. At some point consistent patterns of "failure" in inner city school district after inner city school district must be viewed as the explicit goal not attributable to individual shortcomings.

There is a need to move as far away as possible from the narrow spectrum of conventional education reform both in inner city schools and prisons. People who are being left out of the formal educational process either through subpar academics or no academics at all are going to have to learn in the same way human beings learned for thousands of years, through self-directed learning. That is the long and short of it.

Lacino

Dear Carl,

I must apologize before I get started, but this will be extremely brief.

I am not an educated man by society's standards. I do not have any advanced degrees, nor am I an expert in any particular field. But it does not take advanced degrees or expertise to know that the exclusive focus on a person's immediate challenges and disadvantages cannot capture their full impact. Cognitive development, educational attainment, mental health, occupational trajectory, economic success, even romantic relationships, are all influenced across generations.

For example, my foster mother often told me stories about her grandfather and grandmother sharecropping. Stories about her picking cotton as a child growing up in Memphis, Tennessee. She told me about being forbidden from using the front door when she went to the land owners' house, never being allowed past the kitchen, vicious beatings, and being forced to show extreme deference to whites. My mother also told me stories about positive changes in race relations and the social environment when she left Memphis and headed north. However, the move from south to north did not undo the lingering influence of generations of racism and trauma on how she thought and interacted with others.

After my mother left the south, she continued to use the side door instead of the front door to enter and leave the house. Despite having a beautiful living room, dining room, and sun room, she entertained guests only in the kitchen. When she punished me, she would do so by beating me with extension cords and razor straps. And my mother consistently instructed me to be more respectful of white adults than Black adults. In short, a geographic change did not disrupt the effects and influences of generations of racist ideas and practices.

Now this assessment should not be taken as a critique of my mother's morals and values, or if she was a good person or not, but as a lens with which to view thought patterns and behavior as the product of generations of influences. Looking at a person's immediate challenges and disadvantages tells us little about the cumulative challenges and disadvantages formed over long periods of time. My mother embodied a racist and traumatic legacy and probably wasn't even aware of it, the same way some people are not aware of their racism. So in this sense, when we think about the reproduction of inequality in income, education, occupations, wealth, or cognitive ability, it is not sufficient to focus on a single point in an individual's life or even on a single generation of a family.

I hope this helps in some small but substantial way. If not, I apologize in advance and hope you will push me further.

Your friend,
Lacino

Dear Professor Katy,*

The heat here is unbearable. The housing unit feels like it is one block down and one block over from the sun. Perhaps it should—this prison was built in the late 1800s and was not constructed with any of the modern heating, cooling, or ventilation technologies. From the outside this prison looks like a castle. A Gothic structure that is physically imposing and intimidating. From the inside it looks like a dungeon. Like something out of a Henry the VIII movie. This place really brings the words "archaic" and "draconian" to life.

We, as individuals and a society, have settled into archaic and draconian ways of thinking and acting. Archaic and draconian ways of thinking and acting that assume all situations are identical. Thinking and acting that precludes us from viewing the experiences of both offender and victim as dynamic and something that cannot be addressed in a procedural manner, procedural manners that limit the range of opinions and observations that are considered when trying to determine what is in the best interests of all parties involved.

Assuming all situations are identical or that they can be addressed through rigid procedures means police, prosecutors, courts, and the prison system are not required to listen to individual stories of victims or offenders. I actually see this as a way of controlling the narrative, ways of absolving institutions and systems in our society while demonizing the accused. Sometimes these procedures also demonize victims too. Procedures control the narrative by decreasing what can and cannot be the subject of inquiry.

I think one of the best tools to get offenders to be accountable and assist victims in healing and feeling whole again is to do more listening than accusing. Listen with curiosity, not judgment. Listening to figure out why, and what we can do differently in anticipation that the outcome will be different also.

---

* Katy Wood, another professor with whom Lacino corresponded.

Listening is hard for people who work within the criminal justice system. I mean, if it is assumed that all situations are identical the assumption is also that the criminal justice system is already aware of what the problem is. Therefore the structure, size, volume, and history of the criminal justice system forces our thinking into, as I alluded to, rigid procedures. We do not realize it, but we are unconsciously trying to fit everyone into a rigid box of assumptions, and that makes the outcome of those procedures highly predictable and controllable.

It takes time and patience to listen, something that the criminal justice system minimizes and subordinates to efficiency and standardization. See, the willingness to listen lies in the willingness to change. This is what makes listening such a challenge; it often results in the need for change. But when assumptions have been made that situations are not dynamic, why should procedures be dynamic? That leads to another assumption, that procedures should be controllable.

Listening must be the top priority. More important than procedures and predictable outcomes. Listening is most important because the experience of victims and offenders is ever evolving. It is a dynamic process. Even if we end up in a similar situation, how we got there wasn't necessarily the same.

Sounds simple, doesn't it? Well, it isn't as difficult as it has been made out to be. We can do better, but we have to listen to more than agents of the criminal justice system. We have to listen to the people who are most responsible and who are harmed. Tell me what you think of this.

Lacino

"I didn't create this impasse. I had nothing to do with the arrival of matters at this destructive end, as you infer. Did I colonize, kidnap, make war on myself, destroy my institutions, enslave myself, use myself, and neglect myself, steal my identity and then, being reduced to nothing, invent a competitive economy knowing that I cannot compete? Sounds very foolish, but this is what you propose when you place the blame on me or on 'us.'"

—George Jackson[1]

Dear Dr., Professor, friend of mine,

I don't think I am going to spend a lot of time this morning explaining how the generic formula of justifying oppression, by finding defects in the victim of oppression, is a multibillion-dollar industry. A malevolent and dangerous industry encompassing almost every American problem. An industry that has acquired legitimacy and influence, in part, because entertainers and academics, many of mediocre talent, are its paid spokespeople. Spokespeople granted public platforms even when they have no special expertise or experience with the problem they write and speak about.

Finding defects in the victim is so popular, so American, that with or without paid spokespeople we have been conditioned to ask, "What is wrong with him?" "What was she thinking?" "Why would 'they' do something like that?" Then answer those questions in ways that absolve the actual culprits, which, more than likely, is an institution, corporation, or state agency, considering every aspect of our lives is dominated and controlled by them.

So, for example, in Detroit, Michigan, 42 percent of fourth graders are behind in reading and math. No one asks questions about dilapidated buildings, two or three students sharing one textbook, no textbooks, ten (sometimes more) additional desks in the classroom, irrelevant curriculums, teaching models based on teaching tests—not about immediate problems or solutions, metal detectors, armed guards, mini police stations. Instead we are encouraged to confine our attention to the student and to dwell on his or her alleged defects. Pointing to his or her supposedly deviant family or absent father. What?

Let's say for the sake of not arguing that no one in a particular student's family can read or count. Are you telling me the school cannot teach the student to read and count, and do it proficiently? What use is the school? Can you imagine if 42 percent of Google or Amazon's workforce was underperforming? Do you think they would blame the individual worker or immediately recognize there is a company problem? Would they bring individual workers in and fire them one at a time or assemble all the top executives, quality control, industry experts, and troubleshooters to fix the problem? Do you think they will do a survey to assess how many workers grew up without a father in the home? That would be absurd.

It is just as absurd when mass incarceration is analyzed by looking at the individual prisoner instead of asking how is it that America is 5 percent of the world's population but 25 percent of the world's incarcerated people are in American prisons. Instead of asking how Black people, 12 percent of the American population, make up over 50 percent of the prison population. Instead of asking why America tries to incarcerate itself out of problems that are economic and political at base—the product of choices made by elites. The logical outcome of analyzing mass incarceration in terms of alleged deficiencies of individual prisoners is the development of programs that leave the systems and machinery responsible for facilitating mass incarceration untouched. The formula for action becomes extraordinarily simple: change the prisoner. What about changing a society that could have mass incarceration? What about that?

Blaming the individual and absolving institutions, corporations, and state agencies happens so smoothly, has been happening for so long, that it seems downright rational. First, identify the problem. Not in advance of the problem, because it has reached a point where it can no longer be denied or easily explained away. Second, study those affected by the problem and discover in what ways they are different from those not affected. Is s/he Black, no degree, poor, urban, immigrant, something? Third, define the differences as the cause of the problem itself. It is because s/he is Black, has no degree, is poor, urban, an immigrant, something. Finally, invent a response that deals sternly with those "differences." Like monitor those "differences," confine those "differences," neutralize those "differences." And to add insult to injury, the response is said to be done in the best interest of those being monitored, confined, and/or neutralized.

Of course the problems are there. They are there in such proportions I understand why many people feel unsafe. Why people are screaming out for "something" to be done. But the people you cite are opportunists who reap fame, fortune, and national celebrity by denying that racism, classism, and sexism are behind a lot of our desperate living. People who are not in solidarity with prisoners. Who do not help us find ways to be heard. Who do not match their resources with our ideas. Who do not follow our lead. They are given awards and book deals while those who are really with us, colloquially, "those that fuck with us," are marginalized.

And this does not mean prisoners are beyond criticism. Every person is morally responsible for his or her actions. But George L. Jackson was right. I did not colonize my neighborhood. I did not kidnap the jobs that allow people to do more than just survive. I did not make war on my life chances, life chances sociologists were debating before I was born. I did not destroy four hundred years of informal ways of solving personal and community problems. I did not enslave my neighborhood to corporations with political power so oversized their desires become political realities to the detriment of my reality. I did not use my father and uncles, mother and aunts to build wealth for Ford, Chrysler, and General Motors just so they could go from three to two to one to no shifts. I did not gerrymander and reform away the vote. And then, being reduced to irrelevance, dispose of myself for fifty-two to eighty years.

I let you keep me longer than intended. I could have ended this letter with George's quote. No more needed to be said. That is one of the things I admire about him. What it takes others entire seminars and books to get across, he accomplished in about the time it takes to wipe the sweat from one's brow. I am working toward that.

You, my friend, must work toward being more outspoken for those of us whose perilous conditions place us beyond the courteous, the politic, even the civilities of political tolerance. We need to hear, sometimes, our frustrations and rage articulated by you all with social standing. We need reassurance that others, not us, are the cause of the wretched circumstances in which we live. Okay? It means more sometimes coming from your mind, your pen, your throat, your hands and feet. Trust me on this.

Lacino

Lisa,

I have received the last two letters you mailed in as many weeks, containing messages from your brother. Thank you for being such a trusted and reliable go-between. It is not humane that MOOC (Massive Open Online Course) officials no longer allow prisoner-to-prisoner correspondence. After two decades of denials, some of my closest friends and more trusted comrades are in here with me but confined at different prisons. When you hear from your brother again, get it across to him that there is no need to apologize for not matching me letter for letter. Convey to him I am not the least bit angry with him. I fully understand the situation— the overall thing that is.

Even though we are both doing time, we are not doing the same time. We have individual situations and problems that are unique to us as individuals that must be negotiated and solved in individual ways. Meaning, while we are both locked in a cell, shackled with policies and rules stripping us of identity-building materials, bloodied but not bowed, our sentences are different, our appeals are at different stages, our support systems are not the same, our home situations with family and friends are different, intangibles we bring to the fight are different, and so on. Just because we are both doing time does not mean we are doing the same time.

I keep this in mind when I calculate what to expect from your brother and the other men around me forced to live in such tight and predictable quarters. This is one of the contradictions that makes prison so destructive. Prison cannot recognize individuals, only "prisoners," a mass who supposedly think and act alike and therefore should be managed and controlled alike. Treating everyone the same based on a mythicized American fascination with "the criminal" is itself criminal because it's a consistent assault on our individuality, identity, and personality.

Also, your brother is not petty, as you characterize him. One of the things I have recognized, not just about prisoners but with people in general, is when people are in cramped spaces, their worldviews are often shrunk down to fit those spaces. For example, when people are penned down in ghettos or packed in prisons, the way they see the world, themselves, and others sometimes shrinks to fit the tight squeeze. And on some levels, this makes sense.

Our minds are so expansive, our personalities are so intricate, our identities are so complex that if they do not make certain mental adjustments, the prison would use violence to force them to miniaturize. That's what Jim Crow and segregation was about—reducing the world of possibilities. Prisons are no different. They not only reduce where one can go and what they can do, but what one sees and hears. Prison censorship is another form of Jim Crow and segregation. Saying it makes sense only means I recognize your brother's limitations as an indictment of the prison, not him.

Rare is it an actual conscious choice to shrink one's estimation of the possible. It is more like a reflex. One of the mind's automatic defense mechanisms. Perhaps somewhere in the pantheon of psychology literature this has been a subject of inquiry? People would go insane constantly bumping up against artificial boundaries separating them from materials commensurate to being more human, or they would be in a perpetual state of rage. I think it is easier for your brother to focus on the few things he has a little control over instead of the world beyond the bars, gun towers, high walls, and razor wire where he has nothing.

Every few years or so, prison administrators bring me back to maximum security prison where prison is narrower, smaller, and more confined. They attempt to put my mind back in this box. Their way of letting me know that writing essays that are viewed by people all over the world, calling into radio stations, being interviewed, being someone that academics and activists consult, and the many other ways I live beyond prison, is not the role of a prisoner. The prison has to manually shrink my worldview since I have no built-in reflex and am not playing defense. Prison does not define me. I am a human being and member of the human family. Anywhere humans are, I have a right to occupy that space and contribute according to my desire and skill set, but there is a price to be paid.

Lisa, it is all bad. Shrink or be shrunk. Few actually fight. Do not judge your brother. Understand and support him the best you can. Remember that I am here to assist.

Your brother from another mother,
Lacino

Dear Professor Shari,*

Generally speaking, people who work in prison are not "bad" people. There are always the sadistic types that can be found in any profession, but that does not make prison work unique. Prison staff are tasked with the bureaucratic management of large groups of people. This does not allow them to interact with incarcerated people as individuals.

When people enter prison, they stop being individuals with individual personalities and statues. They become this sort of inanimate object, a uniformed body that must be controlled and managed. I will cite examples.

The personal possessions of an individual are an important part of the materials out of which one builds a self, an identity, but the ease with which an incarcerated person can be managed by staff is likely to be made easier with the degree to which s/he is dispossessed. The remarkable efficiency with which the prison can adjust to people transferring in and out, or moving to different parts of the prison is related to the fact that incarcerated people do not have much in the way of personal possessions—identity-building materials. Everything I possess can fit into a typical-sized green duffel bag.

So when prison staff find another possession that can be eliminated, they are not doing so with malicious intent. It is bureaucratic policy that makes the running of prisons more efficient. Still, eliminating personal possessions assaults one's identity.

Just as personal possessions may interfere with the smooth running of a prison, so does interaction with family and friends. "Visits" are not viewed as therapeutic or something as natural as breathing. They are looked at as disruptions to the normal flow of controlling and managing large blocks of people. When policies are crafted to limit "visits," it creates the image of prison staff as harsh and coercive when, a line that

---

* A professor at Ohio Wesleyan University who became a pen pal and close friend of Lacino's.

all guards have said numerous times over the course of their career, "I am just doing my job." The problem with this is, the job requires prison staff to fit people in spaces that are not natural fits for human beings. As dynamic as the human mind and personality are, not confining them requires violence, if not physical definitely of the emotional and psychological variety.

The special requirements of the job are carried out without discrimination. It is assumed by prison staff that if a prisoner is incarcerated, they must be the kind of person prison was set up to control and manage. If not, why else would they be there? This assumption is automatic and can never be challenged. At least not to the point where it changes the interaction between jailer and jailed.

Several months ago I refused breakfast and lunch. The quality of food served would bankrupt a for-profit business. The guard told me, "You should appreciate a free meal." I responded, "I would appreciate the opportunity to pay for what I eat." Before walking off he said, "I wouldn't mind paying for you," but he cannot treat me like someone he would not mind dining with. He is compelled by the necessities of the job to read the charge that justified my placement in maximum security segregation and treat me accordingly. He has to, or the jailer/jailed dynamic does not work.

He has to treat me accordingly despite the fact that out of twenty-four years of incarceration, I have no violence in my prison jacket. My behavior is still translated into terms suited to the prison's avowed perspective.

Given the prisoners of whom prison staff have charge, the staff tend to evolve what may be thought of as a theory of human nature. As an implicit part of prison staff perspective, this theory rationalizes activity, provides subtle means of maintaining social distance from incarcerated people, and a stereotyped view of them, and justifies the treatment accorded them. An evolution that does not require concerted effort. Working in prison does not require one to think deeply about it. The same way working at McDonald's doesn't require a cashier or fry boy to think deeply about culinary science or an auto assembly line worker to think deeply about automotive engineering. All they have to do is show up and "do their job."

I think prison staff feel very uncomfortable when they read my essays and other writings. They assume I am being critical of them, when I am not—I am being critical of the situation. Many would like to do their job differently but are just as handcuffed as I am, in a very real sense.

Lacino

Dear Professor Shari,

I too had plans of making a comparative analysis of neocolonialism and American prisons. My notes were thrown away last time I was segregated, so I put off writing an essay. But I can still give you a broad outline of prisoner facilitators, okay?

As prisoners in Michigan and throughout the country begin the grueling process of breathing life back into the prison movement, a process through which we have been slowly moving the last decade, of utmost importance is a cogent analysis of the situation in which we find ourselves. It is my belief that through this process the larger movement for social justice can use that analysis as a blueprint to review and reassess broader movement, actions, and processes.

After nearly a quarter century of being imprisoned, I began to recognize the need for reorientation and reorganization of the prison movement. It appears to be DOA here in Michigan. The strategic and tactical shortcomings over the past five decades were primarily caused by internal weaknesses and only secondarily by the repression of prison authorities and other object conditions. For this reason, a "new" sustained, revolutionary phase and movement must begin with conscious and systematic attention to those internal forces that are the basis of change and development.

I am, or at one time have been, in contact with most prisoners throughout the country who fulfill significant roles in the prison movement. Many have and continue to scoff at the mere suggestion that this kind of discussion should be among the first steps taken in the process of generating greater social activism and of building a new prison movement. But I believe such a discussion is not only necessary in and of itself but also a means of dramatizing the sharp reality of the conditions and the nature of the contradictions between people working within the margins of American society, the American capitalist system, and America's reliance on prisons.

One of the paradoxes in attempting to understand the creations of American prisons and why America imprisons at the rate it does is that research and statistics seem to obscure rather than clarify the inquiry. Research and statistics are not only unreliable in terms of sources, models of calculations, and definitions, but also because prison research and statistics do not take into consideration that the American ruling class has had great experience in distorting and co-opting social movements—for which prisons have historically played a major role.

I know this will seem blasphemous to an academic like yourself, but prisoners are going to have to be their own authorities going forward. Of course it is within our purview to fall back on any research or statistics we independently verify, but our analyses and conclusions are sufficient without them. Most research and statistics sources, models of calculation, and definitions are designed to obscure why America leads the world in imprisonment. For example, just take a look at official crime statistics. The seven or eight categories used to measure crime say more about the desperation of poor people than they do crime.

It would seem logical to conclude, as many do, that American citizens are better off than ever before in this rapid technologically advancing and generally open society. But the fact is that in a myriad of ways millions of people are not. For example, menial jobs and low income has decimated the ranks of the middle class; tens of thousands of college graduates cannot find work commensurate in their particular field of expertise; personal debt is at an historical high; and despite the best efforts to eliminate race-based oppression, it returns time after time in different guises.

Prisons are represented to the public as necessary institutions designed to incapacitate lawbreakers and keep society safe. In reality they function more like storage dumps for those who fall into the above categories, and those who have no place in the political economy. All the official denials and aspirational rhetoric in the world cannot mask the deteriorating economic reality of the last half century. Millions of Americans have been forced out of the economy. Many of which are or who will be imprisoned.

If all these conclusions are valid (we are our own authorities out of necessity), then it is precisely this possibility, no, probability of a permanent underclass being forced into prison that necessitates a form of indirect rule.

Prisons have swelled to where the guard-to-prisoner ratio is something like one to fifteen. Guards cannot rely on force alone to control prisoners. There have to be other assurances. Other levels and safety valves. Therefore, prisoners are "recruited" to assist in the process. It requires varying degrees of prisoner cooperation and collaboration. But this alliance minimizes the frequency with which they resort to the brute force necessary to preserve control. From this a working definition and analysis of prisoner facilitators can proceed.

In America today a program of domestic neocolonialism is rapidly advancing. It has largely gone unnoticed because it is taking place behind the high walls of American prisons. And because neocolonialism is commonly associated with providing raw materials for people whose origins are in some other country, it is not associated with prisons and prisoners. It was designed to assimilate prisoner leaders and abolition rhetoric into the prison machinery while subtly transforming the abolition program for social change into a program which in essence buttresses caging us for part or all of our lives.

The MDOC is constantly faced with the dilemma that preoccupies DOCs in all fifty states: the bureaucratic management of large numbers of prisoners. Every prisoner must do exactly what is commanded of him or her, even if the command is silly or dangerous or the prisoner/guard dynamic does not work. The most effective management model then for prison authorities, a numerically small group to control prisoners, a numerically larger group, is to set up an "elite" within the prison group who are willing to champion the ideas, programs, and attitudes of the prison. Such a management model has been effectively achieved with the creation of "prisoner facilitators."

As a class, in Michigan, prisoner facilitators were created in the early 1990s. Mostly older prisoners, usually lifers, with significant time served

who have been shaped and coded by chronic anxiety about the consequences of breaking rules. Consequences that ranged from ridicule,
vicious ribbing, and suspension of privileges to moderate and sometimes
severe corporeal punishment. Prisoner facilitators were made necessary
by the rise of modern large-scale prisons, with the concomitant requirements of control and protecting the status quo within the prison. Said
another way, prison authorities' efforts to micromanage the daily activities of forty-five thousand men and women in a restricted space with
finite resources is optimally realized when prisoners act, in effect, as the
tacit representative of the prison.

Seen as traitors by some prisoners, prisoner facilitators consist of, but
are not limited to, head porters, clerks, assignment foremen, warden foremen representatives, program liaisons, religious leaders, and even some
gang leaders. The task of this class of prisoners is to ease the adoption
of behavior modification techniques and facilitate programming to that
effect.

Because of their popularity among fellow prisoners, reputations as
former hustlers and tough guys, work assignments that give them imaginary power to "make things happen," educational achievements, sometimes opportunism, these men and women are recruited to represent the
facility and be guard proxies. Through near total obedience in action
and spirit, prisoner facilitators have effectively become appendages of the
prison. In the vernacular, model prisoners who possess an intimate kind
of involvement with the formal running of prison. They have adopted
the "official" or guard view. Their talents, skills, and enthusiasm are
placed at the disposal of prison authorities. In exchange for serving as a
model to other prisoners, prisoner facilitators receive a small number of
clearly defined rewards and privileges. For example, guards overlooking
minor rule infractions, extra time out of cell, confiscated property from
other prisoners, privileges so minor (like a cup of coffee) to reveal the true
depths of prisoner deprivations.

When this same process occurs between a major power and an
underdeveloped country, it is readily recognized as neocolonialism. I use

the term to describe activities in prison because, as should be by now quite evident, the creation of prison facilitators is analogous to corporate penetration of an underdeveloped country. The methods and social objectives in both cases are identical.

In all fairness, prisoner facilitators are frequently more than the product of capitulation but firm conviction. Many have faith that if they buy into behavior modification schemes it will expedite release and improve their odds of successfully transitioning back to society. This sounds commendable, but close scrutiny reveals when there is gross disproportion of power like there is in favor of prison authorities, most, if not all, interactions between guards and prisoners will be accessory and gratuitous, guaranteeing that "rehabilitation" will be in the interest of the prison.

Rehabilitative rhetoric is used to cover up the nefarious nature of the resocializing process. For example, in 1962, at a meeting in Washington, DC, between a social scientist and prison wardens, Dr. Edward Schein presented his ideas on controlling prisoner populations.[2] He said that in order to produce marked changes of behavior and/or attitude, it is necessary to weaken, undermine, or remove support of old patterns of behavior and attitudes.

Dr. Schein then provided the group of wardens with a list of examples that are ever so present in Michigan prisons today. They are, in part, physical removal of prisoners from those they respect to positively break or seriously weaken close emotional ties, segregation of all natural leaders, the use of cooperative prisoners as leaders, treating those who are willing to collaborate in far more lenient ways than those who are not, and placing individuals whose willpower has been severely weakened or eroded into a living situation with several others who are more advanced in their thought reform, whose responsibility it is to reinforce the attitudes and behaviors desired by prison authorities. All of which prisoner facilitators exemplify.

Following Dr. Schein's address, then director of the US Bureau of Prisons, James V. Bennett, commented that he and the other administrators had a tremendous opportunity to carry on experimentations, and one of the things they could do more of is research, which in my opinion is why most criminology research is suspect, regardless of how academic or neutral it reads. Bennett suggested that they could manipulate the prison environment and culture. Out of that research came the idea of prison facilitators.

With the help of prisoner facilitators, prison authorities have been able to operate without facing many of the problems which once made intimidation and physical force a necessary expedient. Not only do prison facilitators espouse a model of behavior that is at once ideal, employing a sternness sometimes excelling that of prison authorities, but they tend to be leaders among the prisoner population, depriving the prisoner population of needed skills and resources. They also tend to surrender thinking independently of the people who imprison them. They create prisoners who consider behavior with obedience as a baseline behavior and who judge behavior only in terms of being nonconfrontational and what's in the best interest of the prison.

In other words, prisoner facilitators came to pass in Michigan prisons because MDOC authorities had decided to undergo a partnership with some prisoners in pursuit of indirect control to lessen the need for direct control. But the results are the same.

Now, I don't know how much sense this makes to you. I definitely need to work this into a formal writing. But neocolonialism as a concept is alive and in effect in Michigan (and other) prisons. I would really appreciate your thoughts on this and if this at all lines up with what you are writing.

Lacino

Dear Rhonda,

Do you remember the first time you visited me? Afterward I rushed back to the cell to type you a letter while the experience was still near the surface. I asked you a question that you still have not answered: how did I get so lucky to have someone so intelligent, persistent, and committed to come into what is clearly a thorny situation? I do not know how it happened. I do know I appreciate this wonderful feeling I have never felt before. I also appreciate you for assisting me in all the critical areas. You are no paperweight. You are a mountain. Mount Toubkal. Ahaggar. Kilimanjaro. You definitely are no lightweight.

I received the Black Lives Matter response. It was vague. Are they going to partner with us (i.e., Incarcerated Lives Matter) to assist in fostering this dialogue with a larger audience? We need clear ways to define and analyze incarceration so that we understand how it operates at individual, cultural, and institutional levels, historically and in the present. #IncarceratedLivesMatter can help us make sense of and hopefully act more effectively to reduce harm and the assumption that incarceration is the best way to do that.

Just a few years ago, the crisis of incarceration was largely an invisible issue, talked about almost exclusively in abolitionist circles and on prison yards. However, today, it is part of the mainstream discourse, but not in the way #BlackLivesMatter is part of the mainstream discourse. #BlackLivesMatter is mainstream through grassroots organizing and forcing the issue. Conversations surrounding incarceration have been taped and stapled together mostly by elites concerned with mounting fiscal pressures. This is unlikely to result in more than a few modest reforms.

As the incarceration rate grew over the last four decades, so did the political influence and power of those with vested economic and political interests in maintaining the world's largest penal system. It is unlikely such powerful interests will allow incarceration to be significantly reduced, let alone eliminated without a drag-out, knock-down fight. That is going to require getting into the thick of things—the grassroots.

It is important to stress to #BlackLivesMatter that in order to eliminate incarceration, which is leading to nothing but social devastation and the solidifying of a permanent underclass, maximum cooperation and solidarity is required on the part of incarcerated and nonincarcerated people. I would think they understand the importance of building alliances and coalitions. I think you should see if you can get a telephone number so I can speak with them. They may want to hear directly from me?

As long as elites continue to dominate mainstream conversations around incarceration, little attention, if any at all, will be paid to the root cause—marginalization and permanent sidelining of large portions of the population. The same goes for how caging people for part or all of their lives has removed from the community and families the capacity to sustain themselves free of state and corporate domination.

I don't take it for granted that because people protest police abusing and murdering Black people that they are aware eradicating incarceration ultimately requires struggle against all its forms. Diverse coalitions and networks offer the most promising strategies for the challenge.

Make sure you emphasize that #IncarceratedLivesMatter is not looking for #BlackLivesMatter to work for us but with us. The heavy lifting will come from incarcerated people and their families. Our lived experiences—not always, but often—allow us to see more clearly the contradictions between myth and reality and lead to development of critical perspectives on crime and punishment in America. But we would like to piggyback off the #BlackLivesMatter name and notoriety. Those not directly affected by incarceration have important roles to play in building a movement to educate the public and challenge incarceration.

A movement must include a great variety of people filling different roles if it is going to be a mass movement, if it is going to grow. This is one of the many lessons that can be taken from the Civil Rights Movement.

The Civil Rights Movement illustrates the potential of a coalition between disadvantaged groups working with allies across class, racial, and gender lines. Everyone brought their own perspectives and moral commitments to the struggle and willingness to risk their lives. Of course we would probably be further along if both sides had been risking their lives. When we categorically take options off the table, it places us at a strategic disadvantage. But the merging of #BlackLivesMatter and #IncarceratedLivesMatter gives us a similar opportunity today to build coalitions and alliances across many lines.

History illustrates how tenacious and variable systems of oppression are and how dynamic and creative we must be to the challenges they present. As individuals and as groups, our vision can only be partial. But working together brings multiple ways of analyzing the multiple dimensions of incarceration and working toward a world far less reliant on it.

I want you to make note that not once have I used the term "mass incarceration" and don't want you using it either. Some people think the problem is "mass" incarceration, not incarceration. So let's just keep the focus on incarceration, okay?

I am rushing to get this in the mail to you. If I failed to adequately answer all your questions, come again. As quick as an opportunity appears, they disappear too. So let's put this idea back in rotation quickly.

Together we accomplish more,
Lacino

Comrade,

I thought we went over this before? And because I am certain we have, this will be brief. I received six letters along with yours today. Everyone will have a letter back en route to them tonight. Tomorrow I am going to do something I have not done in over a year—take a day to relax. Do nothing at all. Sleep. Maybe catch a movie. But I will not be reading and writing.

We established early in our correspondences that we do not live in a world of absolutes. There can be multiple reasons or explanations for a single action. And all of them can be true or partially true. Therefore, prisoners like myself who opt out of the administrative model aren't necessarily doing so for negative reasons. So before we condemn all those that "act out" or "raise a little hell," let's look deeper to see if there is anything else there, okay?

The prisoner social system, which some sociologies call "the mix," often provides a milieu where prisoners can avoid the devastating psychological effects of internalizing the administrative agenda. Which obviously is a failure. Nationally there is a 70 percent recidivism rate within the first three years of release. Whatever the prison is pushing, I want no part of it. And that does not make me incorrigible or a threat to the larger society.

In effect, the prisoner social system—fraternizing with those who are going through what I am going through rather than becoming an accomplice in my oppression—permits me to reject my captors rather than reject myself (i.e., act out the role of the perfect inmate). The perfect inmate is a shell of him or herself. In this respect, the prisoner social system can be therapeutic. It is the only place I can talk freely, keep secrets, and genuinely laugh, and sometimes the bonds are enough to run strikes and insurrections. However, the latter two are exceptions, not the norm.

Not every prisoner in "the mix" operates there exclusively the way I do. Many prisoners take the tack of what some call "playing it cool."

This is a somewhat opportunistic combination of embracing the perfect prisoner model and quasiloyalty at the same time in order to maximize the chance of not being harmed by either group. An adaptive technique. You should remember, prison is not a very nice place.

What would you do if it were you? Probably anyone who has never been in a similarly doomed position cannot realize the humiliation of being told, "This is where your best thinking got you, so let us think for you." You cannot realize what it means for this to constantly occur. Most prisoners are just trying to survive and get out in one piece.

Surviving for me, in large part, means exiting prison with my self-worth and dignity intact. Being my own person. Not having the prison become my brain. It's bad enough I am forced to request toiletries or permission to execute activities my teenage nieces and nephews don't need permission to execute out there in the "free world." This puts me in a submissive or suppliant role unnatural for an adult. It opens up my actions to interceptions. The mix is one of the few places in prison where my agency hasn't been completely disrupted.

We should definitely continue this dialogue. We should not dismiss someone because they do not go along to get along. Especially when going along causes the person harm. Sometimes "acting out" or "raising a little hell" are the most therapeutic actions one can take.

Raising "a lot" of hell,
Lacino

Comrade,

I do not justify behavior, mine nor anyone else's. Prison acts to program us to a rigid conformity—mind, body, and attitude. Straitjacket-like. That was the underlying message I wanted to get across. The mix is antithesis to rigid conformity.

Being in the mix may not directly challenge administrators and guards, as you understand it. But being in the mix is a coup of sorts. It allows us to obtain stratifications forbidden by the prison. Obtain stratifications by forbidden means. Forbidden for what? Important evidence that I am my own man with some control of the world around me. Even if that world is prison.

The forbidden possesses a "promised land" appeal. Freedom. Maybe not complete freedom, but in a world of total deprivation, small things mean everything: freedom. Sounds like you've accepted prison as legitimate? Internal order grounded in the use of force? Exercise of total power? Resort to violence to protect the status quo? "Let my people go." Same difference.

Being in the mix is like being part of a subculture. A kind of informal stratification. An informal economy. An informal social arrangement. An informal language. Informal reward system. Informal sequences of indulgences and enticements instead of exaggerated deprivations. What is it about the formal that makes the informal necessary? Let's figure that out.

Although being in the mix is ascribed to our alleged criminal predilections, being in the mix is often a form of protest. When sustained, rebellion against the way in which we live. But even if it wasn't—I assure you it is—I yearn to break away from rigid conformity. Make no apologies for that. And if being in the mix does that and nothing else, that's where I will be. History will absolve me the way it absolved Moses when he made his exodus, absolved the French when they resisted, absolved

Gandhi and company when they stopped cooperating, absolved the Pan-African Congress, SCLC. All were "criminals" of their day.

Have you ever stopped to think that the mix may not be the problem, that the problem may be our storytellers and the stories about prison they are narrating?

Lacino

"A citizen disillusioned with politics and with what pretended to be intelligent discussions of politics turned its attention (or what had its attention turned) to entertainment, to gossip, to ten thousand schemes for self-help. Those at the margins became violent, finding scapegoats within one's group (as with poor-black on poor-black violence), or against other races, immigrants, demonized foreigners, welfare mothers, minor criminals (standing in for untouchable major criminals)."

—Howard Zinn[3]

Dear Comrade,

Where did you get this quote from? Whoever wrote it, I like what they are saying. I would like to read the actual essay it was excerpted from. If it sustains this level of critique then I should be able to make good use of it. Now on to what you wrote.

I have noticed in your correspondence you frequently make mention of the way the government behaves as being a "crime" or "criminal." For example, allying the United States with right-wing tyrannies abroad. Wars of choice. Calling murder collateral damage. Listening to everyone's phone calls. Being the muscle for corporations. Protecting corporate wealth and power. Transferring wealth from workers to elites. And the list goes on.

I have definitely noticed this type of language used more and more by the left to describe abhorrent acts committed by the government: "Bush is a war criminal," that kind of thing. I know this is intended to get the point across that the state only penalizes people at the bottom of the social structure while people who commit atrocities on grand scales aren't prosecuted or held accountable. Still, there is something that bothers me about this.

"Crime" is a political term. Something that is prohibited by the state. The concept of criminal is meant to dehumanize or at least pigeonhole a person as being "something" that is corrupt, crooked, maladjusted, or in need of disposal. This can easily be demonstrated just by asking someone to tell you what they believe should become of criminals. The answers will range everything from banishment to execution. My point is, when someone uses the word "crime" or "criminal" to describe the actions of the state, or elites, they aren't just slamming them and their actions, they are also increasing the currency and the integrity of the concept of crime.

I have ditched that word from my vocabulary. At least when denouncing something or someone. In order to have "crime," you must have police and prisons. You must have a static, unmovable "law" that is imposed. I envision a world without police, without prisons, without social-structural violence, without injustice, and without privilege, the sources of counter-violent acts by individuals. Police and prisons precede rather than follow harmful actions. If we can eliminate conditions that produce harm, we can eliminate the need for police and prisons.

Just calling the state or elites criminals doesn't get at the heart of the problem—social structures and human relations that obstruct fulfillment of inherent human needs and consequently interfere with individual and social development. Instead of perpetuating the concept of crime and the dehumanizing responses associated with this concept, can we, in the process of assisting people deal with conflicts small and big, also overcome the conditions that influence people to think that police and prisons are solutions to problems that are political and economic at base?

Accordingly, we must devise and implement concepts and corresponding language aimed at facilitating the emergence of critical consciousness that induces changes in people's actions, interactions, and social relations. Moving toward a society that isn't saturated with police and riddled with prisons requires transformation of the status quo—reproducing language into status quo-challenging language—critical consciousness. Therefore, we have to facilitate the spreading of such critical consciousness by dialogical, counter-educational processes. This includes the words we use to describe what we want to get rid of and what we are building.

When we interact our actions and communications can either conform to or challenge the status quo and prevailing patterns of human relations. When we speak in accordance with "normal" language and terms, we reinforce, even if it's just by implication, the existing social order and its "common sense" analyses and responses. On the other hand, when our words and actions transgress the ranges of normal communications, we create opportunities for reflection for the emergence of critical consciousness on the part of others with whom we interact.

People ask me all the time why I used a particular word or term to describe something, so I know there is something to this. I am eager to know what you think about this.

Your friend,
Lacino

Rhonda,

I only have a few minutes to get this ready for the mail. I just returned from the Are Prisons Obsolete? workshop, hosted by the University of Michigan-Dearborn campus. The past three days have been wonderful, all things considered. It is the closest thing to university life I have experienced. And I will have you know, I did not give any of the professors a break. I do not think they were ready for some of my insights. They gave me some of my best face-to-face debates to date.

During one of the bathroom and refreshment breaks, I spoke with one of the professors from Ohio State. There were three in attendance. Others were from Wisconsin, Pittsburgh, Illinois, and different parts of Michigan. The professor from Ohio State and I hung back in the gym where most of the workshop took place. We sped read through an essay he brought with him: "Schools, Prisons and the Social Implications of Punishment," by a Californian professor named Pedro Noguera.[4] The essay recounted Noguera's tour of an elementary school in Northern California. The purpose of the tour was to learn more about ways that school was implementing a grant to increase social services for students from poor neighborhoods.

As the tour was coming to an end, Noguera wrote that he and his guide, the assistant principal of the school, passed a boy in the hallway no more than eight years old. The assistant principal pointed at the child, shook his head, and said there was a prison cell in San Quentin waiting on the boy. Surprised by the observation, Noguera asked the assistant principal how he could predict the future of such a young child. He replied that the boy's father, brother, and uncle were all in prison. In fact, he said, the whole family, with the exception of his elderly grandmother who cares for him, is nothing but trouble. He could see in how he behaves that it is only a matter of time before he ends up there too.

The two of us were off in a corner reading this by ourselves. I was wondering if someone made the very same prediction about me. I was a handful when I was eight years old. Responding to the certainty with which the assistant principal made the prediction, Noguera asked the assistant principal, given what he knows about the young child, what was the school doing to prevent him from going to prison? The assistant principal said that he did not believe it was the school's responsibility to keep the child from going to prison. In fact, he said he was preparing to put the child on an indefinite suspension.

We took some time to discuss how a suspension would not work in the child's favor given the difficulty of his situation at home. This is how a lot of teachers and school administrators think, that there is nothing the school can do but suspend a child with problems. I had to point out to the professor the difference between a problem child and a child with problems. A child with problems can, with the proper guidance and information, work things out. A problem child is someone in whom the school does not have confidence; the school does not recognize the child's potential. The school shifts from teaching to custodial care and discipline.

A larger quantity of data on the expectations and attitudes of teachers (e.g., their estimates of the academic potential of students, how many will drop out, how many will graduate, etc.) points to the main dynamic of the school-to-prison pipeline, the belief that some children are essentially uneducable because of their background. Students treated as if they are uneducable almost invariably become uneducable.

We continued this conversation with the group after the break ended. To my surprise a large number of the professors in attendance did not believe their expectations of a student played a more important role in a student's performance in school than the community environment. I was by myself arguing against about twenty professors. The most persuasive argument I made was that the school-to-prison pipeline is real. Walking into some inner city schools is like walking into a military compound. Decaying and overcrowded facilities built like bunkers. Metal detectors. Armed guards. Mini police stations. Teachers who act like prison wardens. Discipline practices bearing a striking resemblance to strategies used to punish adults. Those most frequently punished in terms of race and gender and socioeconomic status look a lot like smaller versions of adults punished with incarceration. They had no counterargument for these points.

In some schools students are not being taught anything worth knowing. They are just disciplined and punished, and nobody bothers to do anything about it. Some teachers and school security will feel free to viciously ridicule and beat up students and they know nothing will be done about it. I was berated in front of the class a lot and suspended more times than I can count. It just made my life more complicated and predictable: juvenile. The less expected of students, the more they realize the rewards of education are not available to them. The more they act out and rebel, not against learning but against the whole situation of custodial control.

At one point in the workshop, I found myself in the center of the big circle we were sitting in, explaining that right now the American education system is an old house that does not do a good job of educating. Explaining that when remodeling a house, it often requires more than repainting a room or two. Sometimes remodeling requires a total gut job. And you have to deal with the dust, dirt, noises, and hazards of tearing down and rebuilding. To stop the school-to-prison pipeline, a total gut job is required.

The solution is not a return to mastering the basics or good test taking. The solution is new pedagogical models and tools. Understanding that "it takes a village to raise a child" includes schools. It is exactly the school's responsibility to prevent children from going to prison. The village is not just the people, it is also the institutions and services. Perhaps teachers as we know them are not even needed. Effective educational models must reflect the experience of students. Therefore, the most effective instrument of educational "reform" is students creating the curriculum they study from.

As the workshop came to a close, a professor from Wisconsin addressed the group and said what I thought was the most profound statement of the entire three days: perhaps students dropping out of school around the country are right, not teachers and school administrators. Students may not have worked out elaborate educational treaties, but they understand from a young age that for many of them education as we know it leads nowhere. Not even to the mines and factories. Students are not fooled by the various euphemisms used to disguise custodial control as scholastics.

A lot of students hate school, hate teachers, hate anything that seems to impose on them humiliation and unworthiness. Because they are not respected as human beings. Because they are sacrificed in the machinery of efficiency and expendability. Because their dignity and potential as human beings is being obscured and ignored in terms of educational irrelevance. Because schools more and more often lead to prison.

Look at me, I said this was going to be quick. Needless to say, the workshop was a great experience. Later in the week I am going to write an essay about all of this. Take care. Last call for mail was just announced.

Yours,
Lacino

Dear Rhonda,

When you entered the visiting room, you looked like a warm scoop of peach cobbler—my favorite. No, a double scoop with a scoop of vanilla ice cream melting on top, running down the sides, a little messy-like. You looked delicious. Made me hate this situation that much more. It is times such as those that I won't forgive. That someone has to answer for denying me a little peach cobbler and vanilla ice cream.

It frustrated me also that we had to share that corner with two other visiting families. But you can't say that the guy sitting to our left who you kept saying was "out of his mind" did not make the visit memorable. I am glad you got to hear some of his perspectives. Ask me, he wasn't "out of his mind" at all.

We can learn a lot about prison if we simply listen to the people in prison. Not just the so-called exceptional prisoners, the ones who keep their face in a book all day or speak grammatically correct English, though they should be consulted too. I suggest speaking to any prisoner. We all know that the poorer you are, the more likely you are to end up in a prison cell.

This isn't because the poor commit more offenses. Who goes to prison and who doesn't has long been a reflection of the American social system in general: the two Americas, one rich and one poor. Racism embedded in both institutions and individual consciousness. The use of victims against one another, like poor whites versus poor immigrants. The lack of resources by the underclass to be heard because money and speech are synonymous in the Supreme Court's opinion. Reforms that change method, not results. He was making a lot of sense.

I especially like what he said about prison programs being weaponized. And even though his choices are limited, "I'm good on the whole playing me like a puppet thing." He's correct. The right to have visitors, to use the phone, purchase commissary (at super inflated prices), to come out of the cell more than fifty minutes a day, they all end up being fully loaded weapons pointed right at us. And if we don't do what the person with the weapon (someone with a made-up title in front of their name) says to do, some privileges we have die.

None of the prison programs are ours. Everything is treated as a projectile that can be used to make us act in ways contrary to our best interests. If we don't the program is taken away. The result is insecurity. A frustration that keeps eating away at you, though there are many others, like the guy on the visit, who aren't cowed. George Jackson was one of these prisoners. I have told you about him in the past, haven't I?

George Jackson was given an indeterminate sentence of one year to life. Talk about insecurity. Having served ten years of it, he became a revolutionary. He spoke and wrote with a fury that matched his condition: "This monster—the monster they've engendered in me will return to torment its maker, from the grave, the pit, the profoundest pit. Hurl me into the next existence, the descent into hell won't turn me ... I'm going to charge them reparations in blood. I'm going to charge them like a maddened, wounded, rogue male elephant, ears flared, trunk raised, trumpet blaring. . . . War without terms" (Jackson, 222).[5]

Prisoners like George don't last. The prison neutralizes them. George was shot in the back by guards at San Quentin prison while he was allegedly trying to escape. That's the state's story. Prisoners that don't go along just to get along are treated the worst. But I'm getting off subject. I must be tired. I think I'm going to lay down and try to dream about how sweet that peach cobbler is. Dream about a little ice cream running down the sides, all messy-like. I miss you a lot.

Dreaming of you,
Lacino

Dear Comrade,

We cannot be persuaded by headlines that inundate the news and media outlets regarding those charged with sex abuse. If we go by what the news reports, everyone labeled a sex offender has raped their way across the country and back again. Not only do they supposedly deserve a ridiculous lengthy sentence and to be raped while they are in prison (I have never gotten the rationale behind that), but they are to be put on a public sex offender registry for the rest of their lives. I have never gotten the rationale behind that either—DOC affiliation for life?

Just let me deal with the facts first. Twenty-three percent of contact sex offenders were younger than eighteen at the time of their offense. Sixteen percent under the age of twelve. In sex abuse cases against minors, a third of the perpetrators were also juveniles. So-called Romeo and Juliet sex cases, where two minors roughly the same age had consensual sex but one parent or guardian pressed charges, make up nearly another fifteen percent.

This isn't to downplay rape. That's not my intention. Sexual abuse is one of the most abhorrent yet ubiquitous offenses in contemporary society. I am pointing out that while the news reports the most sensational rape cases, we don't realize that the perpetrators of rape are often juveniles. And if what psychologists say is true—that rape is not about sex but power—there are large numbers of juveniles who feel powerless in their young lives and express it through sexual abuse of others.

The sensationalized news most people receive about sex abuse cases is damaging. It gives the impression that all sex abusers are old creepy men sneaking in and out of bedrooms or some coked-up villain jumping out of trees, pulling someone into an alley or a vacant building, and getting their strong-arm on. It clearly gives the public the wrong impression about what influences sex abuse, who is being locked up, what happens while they are locked up, what can be done to prevent these actions, why recidivism is so high (a lot of it has to do with parole stipulations), and why more meaningful, progressive, and ultimately more effective responses to the problem haven't been implemented.

The lack of information has the potential to diminish the quality of life and perpetuate systems of injustice, intolerance, and violence. I want to stop children being abused then abusing other children, equip the youngest members of society with the necessary skills, and send processes to break the cycle of hurt people hurting people. If I caught some old guy sneaking in and out of bedrooms or someone jumping out of trees, my immediate response would probably involve my hands and feet. Just being honest with you. But that would be a totally in-the-moment response.

Individuals who suffer from emotional and psychological difficulties as a result of direct experience with sexual abuse or being swallowed up in a world where they increasingly feel irrelevant and powerless are at risk of perpetuating the very cycles of fear and violence that, more often than not, afflicted them. Unless they are afforded an opportunity to confront the harm done to them, and done to others, where does the cycle end? I don't know the solution, or if there is just one solution. I do know there is a need for healing, peace, and justice.

A restoration and rebuilding of
relationships,
Lacino

Dear Professor Shari,

Have you ever heard of "forgiveness education"? I hadn't until about six months back. A friend mailed me a couple newspaper clippings enumerating some of its successes. I have acquired more literature since then. It appears to be an educational model I can endorse because it prepares and empowers people during their formative years to proactively seek answers to the difficult question of harm reduction and harm repair.

In a nutshell, forgiveness education is a journey whereby children in primary grades begin the process of identifying and managing anger, developing understanding of the future by framing the past, and preparing their hearts for compassion instead of hate. I can see school systems in places like Chicago and Baltimore benefiting from forgiveness education. Prisons can teach it with some modifications. And even though politicians' primary school days are behind them, I would make this mandatory for them. But let me take you back to its origins.

Because both violence and the threat of violence have existed in Northern Ireland for centuries, with a particular danger for youth, in 2002 educators in Belfast created forgiveness education as an antidote to the anger and resentment that often follow violence.[6] By starting with the young generation just beginning school, the hope is that by growing up with the tools to forgive and better understand those that hurt them, they may be able to pass on these tools to the generation that follows, ending cycles of violence.

Places like Chicago and Baltimore and prisons can possibly benefit, but this is generational work, not a quick fix. Forgiveness takes time to learn because it is filled with subtleties—it is not the same as excusing, condoning, forgetting, or reconciling. Beginning in the first grade, Belfast children are exposed to the ideas of forgiveness in a manner complicit with their cognitive development. Through role-taking, learning about the wrongdoer, and viewing him or her in context, children learn and understand that all people, even those that hurt others, have worth.

Children are taught about the inherent worth of all people and to act on this insight by displaying the ethical qualities (i.e., moral love, kindness, respect, and generosity) of acting out of concern for the well-being of another. Can you imagine how different the experience of prison would be if guards were taught this in their academies instead of behavior modification techniques, all of which are predicated on force? How different the prison experience would be if prisoners received a version of this curriculum? Prison can easily be summed up as a place full of hurt people that hurt others.

Throughout the curriculum teachers make the important distinction between learning about forgiveness, which I think we all have learned about to some extent, and actually choosing to practice it in certain contexts. Forgiveness isn't mandatory; it is a tool, an option they put in their "interaction tool box." Perhaps I should coin the term? The curriculum asks the children to become sophisticated enough to think of forgiveness and accountability existing side by side. The curriculum introduces and/ with opposed to either/or frames. Breaks up concrete thinking.

Hurt is inseparable from our human condition. Therefore, skills and tools that help navigate—prevent, if possible—hurt should be inseparable also. Perhaps some of your students can write a grant to study this up close, bring back their findings, and begin experimenting with forgiveness education here in the States? Belfast may one day change the world. At least make a significant contribution.

Relearning to learn,
Lacino

Lisa,

Received your letter yesterday. I am battling a cold, so it sat on the desk unopened last night while I slept. Trying to recuperate. Medical is so inadequate, a common cold can turn into the flu, or worse.

When I read about your nephew getting "caught up in the system," I felt the family's pain. Public schools, child welfare services, prisons, it's all the same BS system. If problems don't exist, they create them. If they do exist, they are complicated further. The family is going to have to come together and fight for your nephew. If not, he could get lost in the system.

Advice other than that? I don't have a lot of positive things to say about child welfare services. My experiences were pretty much all bad. That is not an indictment on the men and women who work for that agency. Most of them are wonderful people with heavy workloads, low salaries, and inadequate training but who go that extra mile, all the time. But no matter how often or far they go, they are incapable of creating safe homes—their mandate—because their adversarial approach—also mandated—alienates families.

Child welfare services are like police and prisons: bureaucratic management and efficiency trumps designer solutions. Nothing in the mandate precedes crisis. They are on the back end, after things fall apart. My mother was catching it from every direction several years before she gave birth to me, at age fourteen. Instead of marshaling resources and support for her, she was blamed for failing to protect me. Worse, we were punished by dividing us. Long division. When someone is in crisis, they shouldn't be branded as depraved, unfit, unsuitable, scandalous, trifling, dividable. Emotionally and psychologically, that was devastating.

As much as we must have such agencies, there should be a balanced approach between child protections and family support, differential response systems that permit child welfare service workers to involve families and community organizations in service planning. The family's voice should be the dominant voice in child welfare decisions and built-in community support. Legal interventions appear to be a pipeline to prison. Seriously. The percentage of men I have encountered while serving time who were in foster care or some other child welfare service program is astronomical. Perhaps someone should study this correlation?

One of the reasons family problems reach crisis proportions by the time there is "intervention" is because families are afraid of state agencies. Police practices. Long division. Exasperation. Pipeline. But let me be clear, divestment is not the solution. It gets under my skin when I hear people push variations of the "pull yourself up by your bootstraps, get off the government titty" spiel. This urges people to accept the fact that agencies like child welfare services are not expected to serve us, or not expected to serve us well. Child welfare services is no handout. Our money should serve us. Should work in our best interests. Listen not dictate. Listening could give child welfare services the type of insights and understandings that could keep families together. Assist families prior to problems reaching crisis proportions.

I know this isn't a very upbeat letter. I want you to understand the importance of staying involved and getting the entire family involved. Getting the church and any other community-controlled services involved. Call my aunt. She could be of more assistance than I can. She's out there with you and knows how to navigate the system. Be looking for her call.

Your brother from another mother,
Lacino

Dad,

I compliment you often as a way of expressing appreciation for all the things you contribute to our relationship, not because you are my dad. I love you because you are my dad. But do understand there is nothing utopian about my love. It does not blind me from reality and does not prevent me from making tough choices. Choices where the rewards often are not in frame.

My love, in general, emanates from the mind, not the heart. It is meticulous, not gratuitous. Cerebral, not sentimental. In the name of love, people do all kinds of shortsighted and harmful things they later regret. That sort of love, the purely emotional kind, is irrational. Doing something without fully thinking it through, without any assurances at all, is not intelligent.

Niccolò Machiavelli, in his book *The Prince*, asked, "Is it better to be loved than feared or feared than loved?" The people whose love I desire I would not want to fear me if they chose not to love me. Machiavelli answered by saying it would be desirable to be both, but since that is difficult, it is much safer to be feared than loved—if one had to choose. Sadly, people make that choice all the time. But relationships predicated on fear are just as irrational as those predicated on love.

His opinion was that people are ungrateful, fickle, deceitful, eager to avoid dangers, and avid for gain while someone is useful to them. They will offer their blood, their property, their lives, even the lives of their children as long as things are favorable to them. But when things are no longer favorable, or even look like they may take a turn, love is often the first thing to accompany that turn, looking for the first exit ramp.

At first I agreed with Machiavelli. The first fourteen years of incarceration I struggled in near isolation. When I was convicted and given a death sentence of fifty-two to eighty years, everyone, including you and my stepmom, simply put me out of mind. You even participated in the division of my things when you were aware they would be needed to finance a defense. I expected it from others, not you. I was hurt and angry. I felt foolish thinking you would help in my defense simply because you are my dad. That you would side with me simply out of a sense of obligation.

I wasn't thinking I wanted you to fear me when love failed to rally you to my side. I did think the thin line between love and hate had been crossed. I prayed to God to make my heart cold because I simply did not want to feel that level of pain ever again. Love requires trust. That means opening oneself to betrayal. And that is how I felt, like you had betrayed and abandoned me.

Still, I love you because you are my dad. Because you are my great-grandmother's grandson. I made a promise to her before she expired that I would always stay with you. That is the only thing she ever asked of me. To love and honor my father. I loved that woman in a purely emotional way. She gave the family a fighting chance when the odds were stacked heavily against you, my aunts, and my uncles. She made irrational choice after irrational choice to give you all opportunities she would never have.

But my love for you is not without limits. I will never relinquish the ability to make decisions based on observation, reflection, and critical analysis. When Machiavelli asks whether it is better to be loved or feared, I ultimately answer that it is better to be intelligent. I will not abandon my obligations to you. But I will not abandon my intelligence either. They can coexist. I cannot allow what I feel to interfere with what I know—anyone trusting only in words and having no other preparations made will fall to ruin.

Perhaps I can explain better when I am free. Until then, just think about intelligence factoring into everything we say, do, and feel.

> *Your son,*
> *Lacino Darnell H.*

"Freedom to create and to construct, to wonder and to venture. Such freedom requires that the individual be active and responsible, not a slave or a well-fed cog in the machine. . . . It is not enough that men are not slaves; if social conditions further the existence of automations, the result will not be love of life, but love of death."

—Erich Fromm[7]

Dear Dr., Professor, friend of mine,

Unfortunately, what you described is not new nor infrequent. For example, several years ago a prominent prisoner advocacy group working out of Detroit sent a letter to thousands of prisoners asking if we could provide suggestions on how the MDOC could trim its budget. This was at a time when legislatures were fiercely debating the financial burden of forty-plus prisons. Debating the need to close several prisons if the budget wasn't trimmed.

I was incensed. I could not believe what I was reading. Why would we "intellectually subsize" our incarceration? At least that's how I saw it. If several prisons closed, it would result in the release of thousands of prisoners. I wrote to the group. I asked that they stop sending out that dumbass letter. I asked in whose interests they were working.

The group responded with a critique, claiming to know better than me what was best. Paternalism? A group that claimed to speak for us took the position that I was incapable of thinking for myself. I knew well that the MDOC was bursting at the seams due to tough-on-crime and mandatory minimum sentencing schemes. That the parole board had been passing people over for things like not showing remorse. How does one "effectively show remorse" in a five-minute interview where mostly yes-or-no questions are asked?

It is not uncommon for groups that claim to speak for incarcerated men and women to be actually speaking for their own narrow interests.

They do not realize that we are not grateful for this type of advocacy. Advocacy of the Dr. Frankenstein variety. Advocacy that fights to keep prisons up and running.

I'm not sold on that group actually being for prisoners. They wrote me that they "are not magicians that can simply wave a wand and make all your problems disappear." I wrote back I was aware of that. The same way I was aware that wizardry did not lead to forty-plus prisons in a single state. The credit goes to the biases and prejudices of economic and political elites. I wrote that we weren't looking to trade in one group of masters for another. We were looking for copartners in building a new and better world. That whatever is done it must be the product of cooperation. But it is difficult to have cooperation without mutual respect. That so-called advocacy group doesn't have respect for us. I know when they wrote me back they wrote everything except I was a black monkey.

I had a friend look into their public filings. I did not see what they have in common with poor people—prison's majority clientele. No one on their board has experienced prison. They do not live in the zip codes police target the most. And I couldn't ascertain from public records who the group is accountable to. The group does not collect membership dues from us, so whoever is funding the group influenced the bullshit they wrote about saving the MDOC money.

They acknowledge in their mission statement that prisons need to be placed under intense scrutiny but do not acknowledge that prisoners are in the best position to carry out that scrutiny. I have other examples, but this is one of the more flagrant. If prisoner advocacy groups are to be successful (I suppose it matters—success by what standard?), they must reflect the realities and aspirations of those they serve. The best way to accomplish this is to work with and take direction from prisoners. If they don't or can't do that, I pretty much know all I need to know about them. Perhaps that is a standard right there.

The challenge for every prisoner is how to survive the experience of prison with our humanity intact. How to emerge from this all-so-real nightmare with the requisite strength and capacity to live. I mean, really live as whole human beings. This is why, at some point, if prisoner advocacy groups are to make more quality contributions to the prison struggle, prisoners must do the lion's share of the work. We need prisoner advocacy groups to be our arms, hands, legs, and feet in the absence of our mobility. We do not need them to be our brains.

The recollection has me incensed.

Lacino

Dear Professor James A.,[*]

Since there is no constitutional right for prisoners to criticize or bring public attention to policies and practices that harm us, the prison has taken action against me. I called into an Ohio radio station and articulated the need to create more educational and employment programs for gang members: transformation through education. The prison labeled me a gang member. They followed that up with designating me a member of a security threat group (STG). Transferred me to a maximum security prison. And no telling how long I will be in solitary confinement.

I put in several law library requests. From what I gather, prison officials do not have to provide procedural safeguards when labeling or designating us members of an STG. So the fact that I am not a gang member means absolutely nothing. According to the United States Supreme Court, the Constitution does not require an STG designation be preceded by due process protections. No opportunity for rebuttal. If prison officials say I am a member of an STG, it looks less like they want me to shut the fuck up and more like they are taking action against a dangerous prisoner.

You are right, I can take this to court, but courts have held that when prisoners "claim" retaliation we must prove that but for the retaliation, the adverse action would not have occurred. So first I will have to prove I'm not a gang member? Just how do I do that? Ask gang members to go on record and say they have nothing to do with me? That's the first burden I'd have to overcome. The prison is aware of that. That's why I was labeled STG first.

I cannot think of why a stricter standard of proof of causation should apply for us than for prison staff. Prison staff put on their pants one leg at a time like the rest of us. And they lie like anyone else. We have less freedom of speech than a free person, but less should not mean zero. When

---

* A professor in Riverside, California, who became a pen pal of Lacino's. Professors reached out to him after seeing his published writing.

we are victims of retaliation for the exercises of what free speech we do have, we should have the same right to a remedy as our free counterparts.

The consequences for designation as a STG are only two noncontact visits per month of one hour each. No leisure time activities. A minimum of two cell searches per week. Out-of-cell movement cannot exceed a total of one hour per day. Ineligible for food packages. Restricted from sending electronic messages. Restricted to five telephone calls per week of fifteen minutes each. Unable to be classified to work or self-help programming. And since other prisoners can be classified STG for "associating" with me, I'm actually restricted from talking to anyone. The opportunity to just stand around in the company of other prisoners has been taken away.

I was told that if I do not agree with what's been done, I could file a grievance. Let me tell you about grievances in prison. Grievances filed through an official procedure are constitutionally protected, even though there is no constitutional requirement that prisons have a grievance system, or that they follow its procedures if they do have one, or that they issue decisions that fairly resolve our problems. Doesn't that sound contradictory?

Actually, grievances were only effective when prison riots and violence against guards were the order of the day. Prison staff would listen and seek peaceful resolutions to prisoner problems back then. But when gun towers, tasers, and special response teams (the prison version of SWAT) became the order of the day, official grievance procedures became obsolete. Official prison policy became "might makes right."

The question remains why prison officials would go to such lengths to prevent me from expressing my opinion that educational, vocational, and counseling programs would decrease violence and increase chances for successfully cutting into the nation's 70 percent recidivism rate? STG designation is being used as a cover to shut down independent voices.

When someone is released from prison, officials notify local law enforcement in the community. This can result in my name being added to some homeland security threat lists, no-fly lists, and other lists I have no business being on for my belief that education can transform lives.

I'm not giving up (many have). I still believe that if people were aware of what is being done in the name of justice, in their name, they wouldn't sit or stand for it. I believe they'd roll out with us. Will you help me share this with others? I really do believe in the power of people and the politics people address.

Lacino

"The challenge of every prisoner, particularly every political prisoner, is how to survive prison intact, how to emerge from prison undiminished, how to conserve and even replenish one's beliefs. . . . To that end, one must know the enemy's purpose before adopting a strategy to undermine it. Prison is designed to break one's spirit and destroy one's resolve. To do this, the authorities attempt to exploit every weakness, demolish every initiative, negate all signs of individuality—all with the ideal of stamping out that spark that makes us human and each of us who we are."

—Nelson Mandela[8]

Lisa,

It seems as if lately all my letters begin by encouraging you not to worry, that your brother isn't crazy, a term I have to get away from using because it is both demeaning and dismissive. But your brother is like hundreds of thousands of men and women locked behind bars, one part overwhelmed, depressed, and in pain, two parts angry, idealistic, and determined to right the wrongs they experience: the use of force and the exercise of total power by prison employees. I am certain your brother has no illusions about the possibilities of "putting an end to the bullshit" simply by "putting his hands and feet on someone." Though I don't doubt the sincerity of his belief that "dropping the planet on them" has a place in a broader struggle to end the "constant intimidation and use of extreme force by prison guards."

Tell him that "taking things to a new level" will be used to discredit his being "sick and tired of being sick and tired of attempts to take away his identity." It will also be used as a pretext for the prison to use greater force and the resort to violence to protect its power to use force.

I don't want to call what your brother is experiencing a phase. It isn't. The painful reality he is responding to doesn't end. Life here becomes a dichotomy. A dichotomy between the inside and the outside. The outside is the real life. The inside is unreal. But after a while this place gradually becomes reality and the outside becomes unreal, eventually getting lost in this world. The entire time he is in prison, attempts will be made to reduce him to a willing participant in the torture Nelson Mandela described in the above quote.

Whatever you do, don't try to make him feel guilty or "crazy" for being angry. Anger is probably the right, legitimate emotion to feel. Frantz Fanon, an astute psychiatrist whose work was ahead of its time, theorized that one of the ways for oppressed people to decolonize the mind is to engage in violence occasionally.[9] He spoke of violence as a way of "cleansing one's self," a safety valve or cathartic experience needed to prevent other illnesses from taking form. I'm talking about psychosomatic illnesses like ulcers due to stress, anxiety, etc. According to Fanon your brother isn't crazy but quite normal. Fanon also writes about becoming deeply depressed, withdrawing into fantasies, and giving in to despair, other common emotions experienced by people in prison.

While your brother's survival of the emotional and psychological abuse that no one on the inside can escape depends on many things: two that can't be inadequate are the understanding of prison and prison's objects by him and the people who support him, and the unwavering support of those that support him. Neither you nor he should take it for granted that you know everything about prison because you've been at this for a while—you don't. Get books by criminologists, penologists, and others who traffic in this misery. Read what they have written. And most of all, get your hands on books written by prison administrators and those concerned with behavior modification theory and techniques. You will be surprised how candidly they write about breaking our wills and spirits. I assume they write so candidly because seldom, if ever, do prisoners or their families (or the general public) consult such literature.

As for unwavering support, just remember that caging people for part or all of their lives isn't normal. Remember that whatever behaviors your brother displays are normal. I mean they may not be normal in the sense of how we expect someone to behave in the community, but they are normal in the sense that abnormal living environments produce abnormal behaviors. Your brother's life revolves around punishments and privileges, the severity of which are largely known to animals. The very notion of punishment and privileges are not applicable to humanity. It is the height of sadomasochism to put someone through this and expect them to smile and laugh as if this isn't an emotional psychological torture far worse than any torture to the body.

Everything your brother is experiencing you will experience also, on some level. How could you not? This is your brother, and you love him. So the more informed you are, the more capable you will be to think clearly about America's use of prisons and how to meet your brother's needs.

And don't write me no foolishness about me getting tired of you. Are you serious? You are my sister from another mother. Together we will develop the tools necessary to understand this madness and how to develop a sense of agency and capacity to interrupt and change it. As long as you need me, I will assist.

Your brother,
Lacino Darnell Hamilton

Dear Peter,*

I just finished reading one of the books you mailed, Simone de Beauvoir's *The Second Sex*, which I mostly enjoyed. I found that it resonated with many things I have noticed and experienced before, especially in my romantic relationships and friendships with women.

Before I read a book, I always check the copyright. I like to know when a book was written. I think it is misleading to judge books by contemporary standards if they were written, for example, in 1949 like *The Second Sex* was. Social conditions and "public opinions" were different then. This was after the first wave but before second-wave feminism. I think that lent strength to the book in that de Beauvoir could write frankly without worrying about breaking social movement taboos.

I don't know how much of the book you read, or if you completed it, but much of the book is about how women behave or perceive the world, having been put in a subordinate role where their intellect is often purposely kept from developing. She says that men are taught to "transcend" while women are kept in immanence. In present time I can imagine some feminists would likely accuse her of being antiwoman because she talks critically about behaviors and attitudes women have. But she always acknowledges that it is the result of patriarchal society. That men benefit from it and often perpetuate it.

It is fashionable nowadays to pretend that the effects of patriarchy are only harmful when they arise in men's behavior, not when they are replicated by women, but she does a good job articulating how oppressive beliefs are internalized by victims as well as perpetrators. One of the weaknesses of the book is that de Beauvoir came from the white middle class. Her analysis has a massive blind spot for people who don't have those backgrounds. But I would say that she wrote in general enough terms that anyone could read it and find some resonance with something—even prisoners.

---

* A long term pen pal of Lacino's.

The more I study and understand feminism, the more I come to believe in the explanatory and political value of identifying both the particular histories and characteristics of specific forms of oppression. For example, incarcerated people are also placed in a subordinate role, like women are. And retribution and punishment are just as harmful when we replicate them in our individual lives (e.g., making a student sit in the hallway alone, time-outs, and banishing children to their rooms until they are told they can come out). From my perspective no one form of oppression is the base for all others, yet all are connected within a system that makes them possible.

So while the overwhelming majority of men in prison aren't committed to eradicating patriarchy, or aren't committed to eradicating racism and classism (the primary ingredients behind incarceration), doing so will require struggling against oppression in all its forms. That includes patriarchy, which makes abolitionism and feminism a perfect fit. Abolitionists can learn from studying feminist analyses, and vice versa, and at the same time highlight the distinctive qualities and appreciate the historical and social contingencies that distinguish one from the other.

Feminism has developed important theoretical and analytic tools for a general theory of oppression and liberation. Simone de Beauvoir's analysis of the ways that the system of patriarchy is reproduced inside women's consciousnesses as well as in external institutions is an analysis abolitionists don't have to invent but definitely need to further develop, including developing a process for naming how prisoners collude in maintaining the jailer/jailed dynamic. No oppressed group is better situated to bring the contradictions surrounding their lives to a head, but they haven't. Prisoners are stuck thinking suffering is a good organizing model. When it isn't. Feminist theories and practices can illuminate the psychological factors that contribute to this paralysis.

Feminist theories and practices also sought to create and enact new, more liberated ways of thinking and behaving. Insights from feminist theory and practice have been fruitfully used by other groups to raise consciousness, develop analyses of psychological and social assumptions and practices of their group(s), as these collude in maintaining oppression, and experiment with alternative practices—they can be fruitful to prisoners also.

It was a good, refreshing read. Thank you for facilitating the experience. Let's work on uniting with all those who are sincerely fighting to abolish/eradicate one of the "isms." At the base it's the same fight.

Together we win,
Lacino

Carl,

You say that the cornerstone of America is democracy? Try telling that to people who have been through the criminal justice system.

If America is a democracy, as you assert, the task of the government should be to facilitate political participation by ensuring that all citizens can vote and that their votes will be counted equally, but that isn't the case. There are over 6 million people who cannot participate in the vote because they have been convicted of a felony, which predominantly affects Blacks since we are the ones targeted by the criminal justice system. My question is what does voting for president or who represents you in Congress have to do with getting caught stealing, carrying a gun without a permit, or using drugs, for example? Does one even remotely relate to the other? Drunk driving is a felony in Michigan punishable up to five years in prison, but so is driving on old tags. No vote because of a felony?

If democracy was actually the cornerstone of America—and I'm not going to argue with you here that pulling a lever every two or four years is actually democracy, because it isn't—how does the cornerstone of the country get taken away for activities that have nothing at all to do with voting? What is even more mind boggling is that the majority of the American population has accepted this practice as legitimate.

Lacino Darnell Hamilton

Dear Peter,

Over the years I have read anything and everything I can get my hands on as it relates to police, courts, and prisons. The more informed I am, the better my odds of not being diminished by this experience are. But what I read today, let me say, surprised someone who has seen and heard a lot.

I read an essay by Zachary Haiden, "When It Comes to Solitary Confinement US Fails Mice Standard."[1] Haiden begins by saying in September of 2014, he learned about a law governing the use of solitary confinement he had never heard of before. To be precise, it really wasn't a law, more like a very strongly worded guideline. Albeit, one published by the National Research Council, an important federal agency.

The guideline says that except as an absolute last resort, solitary confinement should never be practiced. And if it is, there still must be an opportunity to communicate and physically interact with others. All this and more is necessary to prevent negative physical and mental health deterioration, which are well-documented consequences of solitary confinement. Haiden thought this would have been excellent information for him and others working to abolish the use of solitary confinement except for one thing: the guideline did not apply to humans, it applied to mice. Thus, "the mice standard."

Haiden recalled a number of audible gasps across the room as he and others learned of this. Many of the people present had been fighting to end the use of isolation in prisons and jails for decades. And here was this rule that was more direct, more humane, and more respectful of the dignity of mice than any policy for human prisoners anywhere in the country. If they were half as shocked as I was, I imagine they fell out of their chairs when they heard of this. No human standard?

The isolation of people, usually for twenty-three to twenty-four hours per day, without meaningful social interaction can amount to torture (i.e., a form of sensory deprivation). Yet it is one of the most common forms of punishment in American jails and prisons, but there isn't a standard remotely close to the mice standard for humans. It's just another one of those things that make you scratch your head and think out loud, "Where is the justice in this?"

I suppose this really shouldn't be surprising because once a society decides to cage people for part or all of their lives, there are no more standards. Contrary to popular belief, we are living in a society void of standards. Solitary confinement is a losing proposition for everyone.

Lacino

Dear Dr. Lampert,[*]

I want to thank you for the book. I had an epiphany while reading it (Ken Kesey's *One Flew Over the Cuckoo's Nest*). At least that is what I am calling it. That superimposing leadership on people, no matter how well intended, can never play more than a superficial role in their lives. I say an epiphany because as I read it, I could not have been clearer that past techniques of negotiations, discussion, and compromises are no longer consistent with contemporary realities. Professional leaders can no longer control the pace of social change. In fact, they are no longer, if they ever were, leaders. Rather, they now seem to be mere executives or functionaries. They are not best suited to electrify, organize, or mobilize people to action.

This epiphany came while being introduced to the story's main character: "My name is McMurphy, buddies, R. P. McMurphy, and I am a gambling fool."[2] It dawned on me that resistance to aggression, repression, and oppression occurs all the time in all sorts of ways, large and small. It hit me like a bolt of lightning that even R. P. McMurphy, who is dissenting, disorderly, a dropout that goose steps into a mental hospital from a prison work farm and proceeds to dismantle the dictatorship of nurse Ratched (a bureaucratic woman who is the protagonist of the story, who wields a sure power that extends in all directions), is a teacher, social justice advocate, and I will go as far as to say McMurphy also represents a Christ figure.

The McMurphy character helped me understand how even in situations of severe repression, subtle uses of language, gestures, and other aspects of everyday life can express resistance. The book also helped me understand how in a very curious way that the "delinquent's" behavior is healthy, for at least it asserts that s/he still has sufficient strength to rebel and has not yet given in to defeat. McMurphy's promotion of gambling, smuggling in liquor and working women, and demonstratively defying

---

* Professor of Sociology at the University of Michigan-Dearborn, author of *Women Doing Life: Gender, Punishment and the Struggle for Identity*.

the rules at every opportunity were all expressions and acts of defiance and autonomy, acts that helped the other men on the ward gradually perceive their personal and social reality and deal critically with it. I love that book.

From the moment McMurphy enters the ward, which is run as if it is a prison ward, wearing work-farm pants and shirt, sunned out till they are the color of watered milk, his face and neck and arms the color of ox blood leather from working in the fields, primer-black motorcycle cap stuck in his hair, a leather jacket over one arm, and boots gray and dusty and heavy enough to kick a man in two (a real badass), he causes havoc and provides a model of change for the patients on the ward.

Kesey uses the Chief Bromden character, a tall American Indian who pretends to be deaf and dumb for thirty years and has been on the ward longer than anyone else, as the narrator who symbolizes change throughout the story. He is the first person who listens to McMurphy's teachings. I call what he was espousing teachings. Chief Bromden realizes that McMurphy is there to save him and the others on the ward and gradually joins McMurphy and the acutes (patients who have possibility for rehabilitation and release) in open defiance of nurse Ratched.

Throughout his narration Chief Bromden hallucinates about a fog machine and air raids. He relates the imaginary fog machine of the mental hospital to the fog that surrounded him during wartime. This indicates Chief Bromden likely suffers from PTSD which prompts him to lose his grip on reality. On a deeper level his hallucinations represent his mental clarity. Fog comes when he is less stable and recedes when he is more coherent. That is the first noticeable change in Chief Bromden—his hallucinations recede when McMurphy enters the ward.

McMurphy usurps his power to change through charisma. Or as Chief Bromden puts it, "I could watch McMurphy at the blackjack table all night, the way he dealt and talked and ropes them right smack up to the point where they just about quit, then back down a hand or two to give them confidence and bring them along again."[3]

The second, small but subtle change in Chief Bromden is that he decides to go to sleep without taking the little red capsule. Not taking the capsule is a conscious decision to come out of the sleep he had been in. He wishes to follow the imaginative, the daring. He begins to consciously assume the risk of demanding real social change, inspired by McMurphy, who is not taken in by the appearance of the absolute authority and control of nurse Ratched.

"I was seeing him different than when he first came in," Chief Bromden confesses to himself. "I was seeing more to him than just big hands and red sideburns and a broken-nosed grin. I'd see him do things that didn't fit with his face and hands, things like paint a picture at OT with real paints on a blank paper with no lines or numbers anywhere to tell him where to paint, or like writing letters to somebody in a beautiful flowing hand. How could a man that looked like him paint pictures or write letters to people or be upset and worried like I saw him once he got a letter back?"[4]

My epiphany deepened the more I read. I reflected on how men and women serving prison sentences have less to lose by a radical stance and have less vested interest in the system than most other people. It occurred to me that people in prison could lend clear and fresh vision, enthusiasm, and courage of despair to the struggle for social justice. Some powerful voices are being raised in prisons throughout the country on behalf of economic and social justice, but unfortunately, any sustained insight and direction has been muted. To translate those voices into action takes more than the courage and imagination of individuals. It takes the power of society, a large portion of which has come to believe men and women in prison are incorrigible, inferior, and useless.

A definite turning point for Chief Bromden, and the point in the story where I think the significance of McMurphy's defiance resonated most with me, is when McMurphy influences Chief Bromden and the other men on the ward to vote to change the ward schedule to watch the World Series in defiance of nurse Ratched. "Let him vote, why don't cha? Why you want to ship him to disturbed just for bringing up the vote?"[5] One by one the men on the ward begin raising their hands in favor of changing the television schedule, something they never would have done before.

Chief Bromden sees it as McMurphy reaching into the fog and dropping down, dragging the men up by their hands, dragging them into the open. First one, then another, then the next. Right down to the acutes, dragging them out of the fog till there they could stand, all twenty of them, raising their hands not just to watch TV but against nurse Ratched, against her trying to send McMurphy to disturbed, against the way she's talked and acted and beat them down for years.

It is the first time Chief Bromden reasserts himself as a functional human being with free will. It is the first definitive response action, possibly ever, or at least since he stopped speaking thirty years before. From here Chief Bromden continues his pattern as he lays down his mop and joins McMurphy and others in their protest against nurse Ratched for disrespecting their vote and not honoring changing the TV schedule. "Now that McMurphy was around to back them up," Chief Bromden narrates, "the guys started letting fly at everything that happened on the ward that they did not like."

A major theme in the story is the importance of rational choice, the ability that determines one's status as a human being. The status of human being is taken away from them by nurse Ratched and the Combine, a metaphor for the larger society, as every decision concerning their lives down to the minutest detail was made for the men on the ward. Humanity is taken from them until McMurphy, who represents the capability for choice, arrives on the scene.

When Chief Bromden realizes he wants choice and joins the other men in protest of nurse Ratched, his hallucinations of the fog disappear completely. This comes at a cost, however. By making that choice, Chief

Bromden becomes vulnerable. He loses the safety and anonymity of the fog machine for making choices. For wanting to be fully human.

While reading I kept thinking how much this story was just like being imprisoned. How every decision from when to sleep, wake up, eat, use the bathroom, even how and when to think, is predetermined by guards (like nurse Ratched) and a never-ending list of rules (like the Combine). I thought about how the moment we assert ourselves as human beings with the capacity to think for ourselves we become vulnerable to an equally long list of consequences.

The next step toward Chief Bromden's self-realization is his aware-ness of the outside world. "I walked down the windows to one where the shade popped softly in and out with the breeze, and I pressed my forehead up against the mesh. I realized I had my eyes shut. Like I was scared to look outside. I looked out the window and saw for the first time how the hospital was out in the country." What this shows is that Chief Bromden could conceive existence outside of the mental hospital, as he could not before. And McMurphy was the catalyst for his change.

Chief Bromden is perhaps the best example that Kesey gives of the beneficial effect that McMurphy had on the men in the hospital. Perhaps the best example that leadership doesn't always look how we think it is supposed to look—modeled after professionals. Perhaps Chief Bromden is the best example of why the more dramatic methods are likely to con-tinue in order to bring people out of the fog, to punctuate the apathy, alienation, and despair of oppression.

Before Chief Bromden reveals to McMurphy that he can talk, he lies in bed reflecting on his years of not letting on that he could speak and understand. "Wondering if he could ever not act any other way again." Remembering one thing, "it wasn't him that started acting deaf; it was people that first started acting as if he was too dumb to hear or see or say anything at all." McMurphy then presents the idea that Chief Bromden may be able to lift the control panel and throw it through the window and allow an escape, presenting to Chief Bromden that he had the strength to take control and be free.

The more I read, the more it was as if Ken Kesey had a front-row seat to life in prison. I wouldn't go as far as to say the Chief Bromden character mirrored my life, but aspects of Chief Bromden exist in most prisoners who have been silenced by a world that treats us as if we cannot speak, see, or think.

In the final chapter, Chief Bromden realizes all that had happened throughout the story, that it was through McMurphy's brand of leadership that he regains strength and freedom to make independent choices, as McMurphy proposed.

The story culminates in a fantastic victory for nurse Ratched. She ships McMurphy upstairs to disturbed (this is the equivalent to solitary confinement in prison), where electroshock and a lobotomy were performed on him. But the ultimate triumph was the martyred McMurphy. Nurse Ratched saw that McMurphy was growing bigger than ever while he was upstairs where the guys could not see the dent she was making on him, growing almost into a legend. "A man out of sight cannot be made to look weak."

When nurse Ratched brings McMurphy back to the ward so the others can see the vegetative state electroshock and lobotomy had left McMurphy in, Chief Bromden cannot stand to see what had happened to McMurphy and smothers him with a pillow to put him out of his misery. It is then that Chief Bromden chooses to make his final step to self-realization by lifting the control panel and throwing it through the window. He escapes, fulfilling McMurphy's predictions that he had the strength to liberate and reassert himself as a human being. "It's like flying free," Chief Bromden says. "I been away a long time."

Is this the sort of analysis you wanted from me? Through this story Ken Kesey writes how leaders are those persons whom people look to as leaders. R. P. McMurphy, the gambler, brawler, recalcitrant, Christ figure, becomes a leader by encouraging others to take charge of and lead their own lives, to make their own choices. He also demonstrates that there are real, often deadly consequences to asserting human qualities in a world that treats people like automations and that sacrifices outlive those that make them.

One hundred percent, thoroughly enjoyed the book. Thank you. It is a great piece of literature and a tool in the arsenal.

Lacino

Dear Rhonda,

This will be brief. I'm rushing to have this in the mail within the next twenty minutes. I need your help, okay? The editor of the *Michigan Citizen* wants me to write a short essay detailing my journey from bullshit public school education to cell study. She wants to know what makes the cell superior to the classroom. She thinks I haven't done a bad job educating myself.

Now I'm not going to waste ink arguing if the cell is superior to the classroom, both are designed to suppress intellectual growth. Instead, I am going to try to debut Scholars Behind Bars, the concept created by my friend Dennis but fleshed out by me. I hate when people want me to write about my educational accomplishments when educational opportunities are slowly being eliminated in prison altogether.

What I would like you to do is write a brief introduction and send it to the *Michigan Citizen* on my behalf. Enclosed is the basic structure of Scholars Behind Bars. I would like you to briefly explain the importance of facilitating efforts of incarcerated men and women to self-educate. What most people don't know about people who come out of prison better educated than when they entered is the majority have to do it themselves, and it is very difficult to do.

It is one of the all-time great myths about prison—that it is an institution of great intellectual curiosity, debate, and advancement. The people that run prison do not want to have to contend with a prisoner population with critical analytical skills or other intellectual wares. It has always been easier for a numerically smaller group (like guards) to dominate a larger population (like prisoners) when that larger population is uninformed and ignorant.

There are people that come out of prison way more informed, aware, articulate, and so on, but they are usually the exception, not the norm. The things that pass for education in prison usually amount to learning how to make simple rote decisions. Policy makers don't want us exiting prison with the intellectual background to compete with their children for shrinking opportunities in the job market. And they definitely don't want us leaving prison with the capacity to figure out what's really going on, socially, economically, and politically. Prison being the equivalent of college is a myth, generally speaking.

Do not doubt yourself. I trust that you can do this and do it well. And make certain you write both of our names as authors. Who wrote which portions does not matter. What matters is that we take this opportunity extended to me to detail my personal struggles for information and knowledge and instead promote a means to bring educational resources to potentially thousands of incarcerated men and women. I will send the editor a letter under separate cover tomorrow, explaining the same to her. I am certain she will understand.

Sincerely yours,
Lacino

ENCLOSURE

Introduction

Scholars Behind Bars is dedicated to providing postsecondary books and literature to men and women behind bars to (1) assist those behind bars to acquire language to critically understand the tensions, contradictions, fears, doubts, hopes, and "deferred" dreams that are part and parcel of living in confinement; (2) assist those behind bars to place their life experiences in a larger socioeconomic-political framework; (3) assist those behind bars to recognize various spheres of ideological influence in their lives; and (4) assist those behind bars to make the connection between awareness and action.

Given that many men and women who are incarcerated come from backgrounds of relative deprivation in terms of education and most correctional facilities offer little more than GEDs, Scholars Behind Bars will be many incarcerated peoples' first opportunity with "higher" learning—their first opportunity to develop the critical tools to reflect on and understand the way they exist in the world in which and with which they find themselves.

History

In 1994, despite research that shows increased education correlates with decreased rates of return to prison, a long-standing section of the Higher Education Act of 1965 permitting incarcerated people to receive Pell Grants for postsecondary education while incarcerated was abolished. With it went an opportunity for the majority of men and women behind bars to nourish their complete intelligence and creativity.

Around the same time, funding for a variety of correctional-based education programs that promoted self-development were eliminated also, further limiting opportunities for men and women behind bars to expand the scope and depth of their information and knowledge, ensuring that the academic achievement of most people behind bars does not rise above a high school diploma or GED.

Philosophy

Scholars Behind Bars is an evolving set of academic projects that creates educational opportunities for those behind bars. Most importantly, through providing postsecondary books and literature to incarcerated people, Scholars Behind Bars seeks to deepen the conversation—and transform the ways of thinking—about what constitutes a classroom and what it means to meet people where they are and engage men and women behind bars in intellectual pursuits that reflect their felt concerns and questions.

Scholars Behind Bars demonstrates the potential for dynamic collaborations between institutions of higher learning, local schools, libraries, citizens of the public, book and magazine publishers, book retailers, other depositories of information/knowledge, and people behind bars.

Goals

At its most basic level, three broad goals of Scholars Behind Bars are to (1) expand learning opportunities for men and women behind bars; (2) assist men and women behind bars to become agents of their own transformation; and (3) build a network of cooperative and mutually reinforcing enterprises and institutions as the foundation of bridging the gap between men and women on the inside and men and women on the outside.

Scholars Behind Bars aims to increase efficient and creative use of literary resources to enhance the mission of multiplying opportunities for empowerment through intellectual development.

Application

Scholars Behind Bars will purchase books and other educational materials and/or secure them through fundraising and book drives and provide the same to incarcerated men and women.

As Scholars Behind Bars continues working to improve the academic opportunities for men and women behind bars, its success will depend partly on its ability to engage public support for educational resources.

Rhonda,

I wasn't trying to keep anything from you. I was so angry at that precise moment, talking about how asinine visiting procedures are would have ruined admiring how beautiful you looked sitting across from me. Your warm eyes, streaks of auburn in your hair, combed over your right eye (like you wore it in high school), those three freckles on your left cheek, you are intoxicating. I just wanted to inhale you in, not those stupid procedures.

If I ever write a book, no matter what I write about—it could be how to change a flat tire in the rain, something about nothing of real importance—my starting point will be an examination of prison as a destructive social unit. Not enough bad things can be said about prison or are said about prison. We always start with the people in prison, never with the people who created prisons, who operate prisons, or just prison as it exists in a so-called civilized society.

I am living under extreme conditions of physical and psychological compression. Contorted. A top-down force. Bureaucratically arranged from the warden on down. Press ganged. Zero options. Twisted and bent until I fit. Think it doesn't hurt? Ongoing processes that can neither be described nor anticipated by the static enumeration of formal powers and functions. It's not being made up on the spot, but the way prisons really function isn't written down anywhere. It can't be viewed on those reality-type shows where reality is left on the editing room floor.

If anyone believes what they see on television, that I am part of an unindustrious, unintelligent, unresourceful, worthless lot of men who have never learned, can never learn—bullshit. When people work that hard to make people look devoid of humanity, you have to wonder what they are trying to distract attention away from. Power relationships.

The prison has a long history of political violence, a course of action (or inaction) adopted when alternative courses of action are available. Could be available. I am, by and large, a third-class citizen. No citizen at all. Subjected to intermittent atrocities. Probably the most important and strategically placed individuals involved in the problems are the cell-block guards. Consequently, any examination of the prison must make a careful and exhaustive analysis of these highly significant insignificant keepers of the keys.

The keepers of the keys: unindustrious, unintelligent, unresourceful, worthless lot of men and women personally and singly responsible for the custody and discipline of many thousands of prisoners. Protected only by their status as a symbol of power. In order to preserve their status as a symbol of power, the keepers of keys must surround themselves with unrealities about me. The realities of the situation are most unfavorable. The question is: what are the social and human costs of such power? Is it worth it? Is a capitalist social order worth defending at this price?

The prison has developed techniques to exploit me. These techniques have been perfected over the past two hundred years of prisons in America. The prison, the keeper of keys, was contorting just as well then as today because those techniques of breaking wills go back even farther—to the plantation. Everything in nature has a natural enemy. Mine is the keeper of keys. A violent resolution of the conflict now becomes increasingly probable.

Of all the personnel at work here, the administrator, the keeper of routine, is the most diabolical. My life is settled into a pattern. Each day like the one before. Each week like the one before it. The months and years blend into each other. Anything that departs from this pattern upsets the keeper of routine. Routine is the sign administrators are earning their paycheck.

The keeper of routine's title functions as a kind of forgiveness from personal failings. Enforcing security, discipline, and routine requires preempting around the title rather than the person. The prison will support the title whatever the characteristics of the person. Which aren't much. Yes, I was pissed the other day. Before I came out to the visiting room, the keeper of keys told me the keeper of routine wants us to get "naked

naked." That's how he said it. If I did not do it, I couldn't see you. What type of choice is that? He's seen you before. He knew I wanted to see you right then. "Come on, get naked naked." Being told to do something doesn't exempt him. I don't forgive. Since most administrators have been trained in the field of psychological therapies, it would be of interest to determine to what extent getting naked is in harmony with the larger body of social and psychological theory and practice.

They must somehow be brought to the awareness that we are natural enemies. They must be assisted in gaining the awareness that my options trump theirs. See, this is why I didn't want to discuss this. I see little possibility of a resolution that doesn't cause me to contort them. Prisons are dependent on the keepers of keys and the keepers of routine to keep weakening me—at least they try. The so-called breaking down of the old and building of the new. Part of the field of psychological therapies. Very thin on therapy.

I think I'm going to lay down for a while. Close my eyes but not go to sleep. Reflect on the last few days. Later, I'm going to begin that "how to change a flat tire in the rain" book. I won't hide anything.

Lacino

Dear Dr., Professor, friend of mine,

Mail was passed over two hours ago. I received the usual few articles, a couple magazines. The guard just left the cell. He brought me your letter. Said it was stuck down in the bottom of the mail bag. I don't know how true that is. They lie all the time about the smallest things. They think if we knew the truth of what they do and why they do it (as if we don't know), we will take their heads off.

Some will. But acts of violence against guards are rare. I've been trying to figure out why. But it does happen, despite all they do to "keep us in our place." Imagine the type of shit that is done (or has been done) for one guard to about every seventy-five prisoners to keep cracking his whip and for us to not crack back. They lie about that also.

I think a lot about men and women in past generations who stood up when the intimidation and force was more overt. What would they do, right now, today, if they were dealing with men and women who think they can control an average of seventy-five people each who do not want to be controlled? For example, what would Robert F. Williams do?

Have you heard of him? He is one of the forerunners, before the Panthers, before Malcolm, that viewed a good offense as wiser than perpetually playing defense. He is one of the many men and women selectively left out of those ahistorical history books.

Robert F. Williams was the head of the National Association for the Advancement of Colored People (NAACP) chapter in the KKK stronghold of Monroe, North Carolina, in 1955, the same year Emmett Till was kidnapped and brutally murdered in Money, Mississippi. Robert Williams spent his early years working in Detroit factories, where he honed his organizing skills. When he returned to Monroe, he got straight to the business of organizing against the KKK after witnessing them force a young Black girl to dance at gunpoint. He organized the Black Armed Guard, mostly members of the NAACP that picked up the gun.

Three years later, after a seven- and nine-year-old were arrested, beaten, and sent to reform school for the crime of letting a young white girl kiss one of them on the cheek, Robert Williams organized to release the two boys. Which they eventually were, but he had to go. He wasn't afraid of people with an ego that told them they could each control seventy-five other people that did not want to be controlled.

Unfortunately, the NAACP distanced themselves from him. Three years later the FBI indicted him for an alleged kidnapping. He asked a white couple to remain in the house until an angry crowd of Blacks that wanted to put the boot to them dispersed. Kidnapping? Robert Williams fled the country to Canada, then on to Cuba, where Fidel Castro offered him political asylum. It was there that he articulated a paradigm shift. A book called *Negroes with Guns*. In Cuba he broadcast live in many southern states via Radio Free Dixie. In 1965 he moved to China. Three years later he was elected in absentia as the Republic of New Africa—Provisional Government's first president.

While I wonder what he would do if he were here right now, I know the guards would feel he'd have to go. That's why violence against guards is rare. What they feel is reality. And having to go means everything from decades spent in solitary confinement to allegedly hanging one's self from the sink. It doesn't have to be believable. You know, kidnapping? But the official story is the only story given credence. Next time you hear "the official story," search for the unofficial. The person telling it will probably have a hand around their throat. So first there will be the business of breaking a few fingers, or an arm.

I'm going to write you another letter in the morning. I didn't address anything in what you wrote about.

I have to do,
Lacino Darnell Hamilton

"The idea of a Black Liberation Army emerged from conditions in Black Communities; conditions of poverty, indecent housing, massive unemployment, poor medical care, and inferior education. The idea came about because Black people are not free or equal in this country. Because ninety percent of the men and women in this country's prisons are Black and Third World. Because ten-year-old children are shot down in our streets. Because dope has saturated our communities, praying on the disillusionment and frustration of our children. The concept of the BLA arose because of the political, social, and economic oppression of Black people in this country. And where there is repression, there will be resistance. The BLA is part of that resistance movement. The Black Liberation Army stands for freedom and justice for all people."

—Assata Shakur[6]

Comrade,

I don't think you understand. What you wrote is another version of the generic process of blaming the victim. You cannot comfortably believe that "those running around like they are out of their minds" are the cause of what's known as the-school-to-prison pipeline. I have been listening to the victim blamers and pondering their thought processes for a number of years. The process is often very subtle. Cloaked in kindness and concern and bearing all the trappings of statistical furbelows of scientism. But when you strip it all down, it means the victimizer is going to continue victimizing—if we don't put a stop to it.

Have you ever heard the phrase "no matter how much things change, they stay the same"? While we are theorizing and arguing back and forth, Assata diagnosed and offered a prescription for the problem over thirty years ago. Not only do those conditions still exist, but they have worsened. More people are poor, homeless, and unemployed (or working dead-end jobs). The same people are filling up the jails and prisons. Poor medical care is no emergency room (crisis) health care. And the public schools are deliberately miseducating. We need to begin calling things like they are.

We must challenge those who blame children caught in the school-to-prison pipeline for their own miseducation. Challenge every way it is said that they carry a scanty pack of intellectual baggage as they enter the school. This is just another way of trying to get us to focus our attention on the child, dwell on all his or her alleged defects. You don't blame the victim, you blame the oppressor.

I mean, since when does the oppressor educate the oppressed—to solve their problems? Assata used the word "oppression." That is the lens through which the school-to-prison pipeline must be analyzed. The term "oppression" encapsulates the fusion of institutional and systematic discrimination, a complex web of relationships and structures that shade most aspects of life in society. It's bigger than personal bias, bigotry, and prejudice.

People that appear to be out of their minds right now will be the first to resist when they realize their problem isn't the guy down the block, around the corner, or the next neighborhood over. When they realize they are going from the school to the prison because of oppression, it's just a matter of time before they get wise that punching and kicking and drawing down on each other isn't the answer. But until then, we can't present this phenomenon in simple descriptive terms with our problems unrelated to other problems and none related in any meaningful way to the victimizer.

That's why so much energy goes into that whole "stop acting like a victim" spiel. I agree. It's time to stop letting people abuse us. But what's behind this spiel is if the victimizer can get us to stop acknowledging our oppression, that we are victims, they will not be acknowledged as victimizing us. You can't have a victim without a victimizer.

The concept of the Black Liberation Army (BLA) will rise again. "Where there is oppression, there will be resistance." This is why schools don't educate. When someone possesses the analytical tools to figure out what's really going on, they can also figure out how to stop playing defense. They figure out they don't have to react and be on the back end of a problem. They realize they can take the bull by the horns and ride it to the ground. That's why schools don't educate. It's a form of offense initiated by the oppressor.

I'm not going to run this into the ground. I'm going to assume that you get it. Now we have to get on with building around stopping the school-to-prison pipeline by building around offense.

Rebuilding to win,
Lacino

Comrade,

I don't see the rise and growth of gangs in Michigan prisons the same way you do (i.e., "just some bullshit"). Most of the men entering prison do so angry and confused, with no meaningful identity. They join gangs in search of something bigger than themselves, some sort of purpose and direction. Some join for protection—strength in numbers. What they find is other men angry and confused like they are. Men who also lack meaningful identity. Without the skills to ascertain what they are in search of, they become involved in a bunch of bullshit, but the gang isn't just some bullshit. Do you follow?

Those guys are trying to organize themselves. But because they are doing so without understanding, instead of eradicating ideas and feelings within themselves that aren't beneficial, they perpetuate them. They are struggling to find substance and worth, affirmation and status, using their own devices. But those devices are lacking. To explain the rise and growth of gangs in Michigan prisons solely in terms of "some bullshit" is a serious error. It's dismissive of the depressive realities of their lives. It throws the baby out with the bath water. An intellectual shortcut.

When I defected from the Melanic Islamic Palace of the Rising Sun, which operated more like a gang than a religion with Black nationalist principles, I could see more clearly from the outside than I could as a member. At first, I was just bitterly criticizing the group. Mostly the leadership, the seven men that controlled the other fifteen hundred members. I looked back and saw nothing of quality and health added to my life. I wanted to box with all seven of them. But they didn't know any better. No matter how intelligent I thought they were, because they could better articulate tensions, contradictions, and doubts than I could, they were just as ignorant and lost as I was.

I don't subscribe to all that rhetoric about growing up in the ghetto or without a father being the reason for this form of organizing. Certainly some attention should be given to a marked improvement in the physical and aesthetic side of the neighborhood, and every member of the neighborhood has responsibilities and owes a debt to his or her family. But the real problem is, there is no sustained program. If people are going to organize, there needs to be a sustained program to strike at the very roots of what makes substance and worth, affirmation and status, another privileged commodity.

Like you I constantly think about starting something new, fresh, and relevant. But when I lay down and stretch all the way out, flat on my back with my hands behind my head, fingers locked, staring up at the ceiling (I seem to do my best thinking from this position), it comes to me that new groups sprout up every day. Some well funded, fully staffed, and armed with best practices. But what about organizations and organizing models that got us through chattel slavery, Black Codes, Jim Crow, dogs and fire hoses, the riots?

When the privileged classes have an organization or organizing model that works, they stick with it. They have institutions that trace back to the Revolutionary War. While at the first sign of adversity, any attack from the system, or attack from within, we abandon what we have. What happened to the UNIA? It was the biggest Black nationalist, pan-Afrikan organization in the history of the United States. What the hell happened to it?

Everyone loves Malcolm X nowadays. He is an American icon. His face is on stamps, all sorts of apparel, but the organization he started, the Organization of Afrikan-American Unity, is as dead as he is. Perhaps if these organizations were still around, these young guys would join them and not gangs? Where are the institutions dedicated to the legacy of Reverend Henry Highland Garnet, Monroe Trotter, Martin Delaney?

I agree that the bullshit needs to stop, effective immediately. But if anything more than the displacement of symptoms is to be achieved, we can't just dismiss people and keep starting over. We have to find what works and stick with it.

Standing on the shoulders of giants,
Lacino

"Believe me, my friend, with the time and the incentive that these brothers have to read, study and think, you will find no class or category more aware, more embittered, desperate or dedicated to the ultimate remedy—revolution. The most dedicated, the best of our kind—you will find them in the Folsoms, San Quentins, and Soledads. They live like there is no tomorrow."

—George Jackson[7]

Dear Comrade,

It would be a mistake to view me being sent back to solidarity confinement as anything other than the MDOC using its asymmetric power to ensure it always controls the situation here—every situation.

At least since the 1950s when California prisoner Caryl Chessman launched a tireless legal and literary assault on the California prison system from his cell at San Quentin, what evolved into a series of bestselling memoirs, prison systems in every state have been on the lookout for prisoners who might emerge as public figures and put the prison system's brutality on trial, unite other prisoners in open confrontation with guards, and rally the public to the prison movement.

There are state and federal committees, subcommittees, a myriad of political formations repeatedly predicting that prisoners will soon rise up. Lesser penalties and abuses than those prisoners endure have been the stuff of revolts and coups. I don't think I can ever describe just how tight it is in here. How asphyxiating it is. Eric Gardner. I can't fucking breathe it's so tight.

When I first began writing to educate the public, I wasn't certain the public would pay attention. But I could see in which direction things here were headed. When you watch the news or read in the paper that the state legislator is having a difficult time balancing prison spending, you may think this is just a matter of mathematics, and it is. The state legislature is in the process of subtracting something essential from us (e.g., two opportunities to see family and friends per month instead of seven). Could you imagine only having the "opportunity"—it doesn't mean you will—to see your family and friends two times per month for an hour each time?

When you read that a guard was frightened because a prisoner yelled after having mail thrown away or having their release date incorrectly calculated, for the fourth time, those sorts of stories may appear benign to you, but I know it signals to those who speak in dog whistles that pepper spray banned by the United Nations, higher voltage tasers, and more armed guards are coming—if they aren't already here.

Writing for a larger audience was part of a larger effort to establish contacts and support for whatever measures we take to hold on to and grow our humanity. Without support from the public, it will be nearly impossible to put a stop to this and to come out more human. I am interested in becoming more human, not surviving. The majority survive, but their humanity doesn't.

When prisoners emerge as public figures or figure out ways to develop dialogue with members of the academy or media or on rarer occasions, policy makers, there is always the danger we will appear human. The danger we will not fit the cartoons and caricatures carefully crafted to denigrate us. If what we experience, which takes you and every other member of society milliseconds to know you'd never want to experience, no longer fits what people think they know about us, the public finds it has no reason to refrain from building up involvement with our struggles and fights.

Prisons are not built way out in the boondocks to prevent escape. The same security measures that went into the construction of Guantanamo Bay go into every jail and prison. They are built in the middle of nowhere to keep the public from riding by and wondering what type of massive deprivations are taking place. Out of sight, out of mind. Social intercourse between the public and prisoners means the public may come to view our desperate acts of being more human as reasonable. View our desperate actions as responsible.

I have been sent to solitary confinement to prevent taking part in that. But we can't let this be effective. I'm not going to shut up. I need you to help. Act like a megaphone. "Act like there is no tomorrow."

Desperate and dedicated,
Lacino D. Hamilton

Rhonda,

I assume you know me better than anyone else. Not simply because over the years you've allowed me to come to you with both my good and my bad (without judging me), but you've been a consistent presence in my life since the age of ten. You've had the up-close-and-personal, panoramic, high-definition view of how I get down. A lot of which I'm not proud of today. But you've been there through it all and have not abandoned me.

However, the letter I read yesterday, where you caution me "not to try to make up for lost time when released," I'd say you don't know me at all. What lost time? The time spent here in prison? Yes, it's been nonideal. But what do you think I've been doing here, losing time? Stop it.

Among most incarcerated men and women, there is a strong feeling that time spent in prison is time wasted, or destroyed, or taken from their life. It is time they write off. Something that has been "done" or "marked" or "put in" or "pulled." Time in prison is something its "doers" have bracketed. Time stops when they enter. No degree. No marital relations formed. No baby making. No mortgage. No anniversaries.

They think in terms of "doing time." Not in terms of what they are doing "with" the time. There is a big difference. They feel that while incarcerated they have been exiled from living. A long sleep. A demoralizing influence on them. I think this is the basis for so many incarcerated people developing a story. A line. A sad tale. So much self-pity.

This sense of dead-end heavy-hanging time accounts for the premium placed on "killing time." All sorts of unserious pursuits (e.g., card playing, horseshoes, mindless TV, "gay for the stay," prisoner-on-prisoner violence, prison programs) make them oblivious for the time being of their actual situation. Then, like magic, supposedly time resumes when released. Are you getting where I'm going with this?

I have got something from time spent in prison that not everyone does. Time to read. Time to observe. Time to reflect. Time to analyze. Time to develop my mind. Prior to prison I had never read a book from cover to cover. My life wasn't based on knowledge and a command of facts. It was all about wits. All will and sheer determination. But that changed when I discovered books.

I started off in the county jail with books like *Whore Baby* and *Kenyatta's Revenge*. Old-school hood novels. When I entered the Michigan prison system, soaking up the Black nationalist tenor of religions—the primary organizing mechanism—I soon found all the Black nationalist classics from the 1960s and 1970s. It did not happen overnight, but along with other contributing factors, I was able to bring some understanding into my life.

I invested a lot of time searching bibliographies of the books I was reading for source material. I discovered the social sciences: sociology, political science, economics, social planning, policy making, war. Time in prison was flying by. I read from the time the lights came on at 5:30 in the morning until they went off at night and I could no longer see the words on the page. And one day it hit me. I needed to invest more time studying my own experiences.

Hugging the block. Bending corners. Twisting. Watching it pile up. The more I read the social sciences, the more it occurred to me that the most respected analysts were writing about other peoples' lives. They didn't personally possess the experiences, but I did. Experience taught me to cut out the middle man. Economics 101. I elevated my experiences above those I was reading about. It was time to write down significant events from my life. Invest more time in me. Past. Present. Future. No time has been lost. Time has been invested.

When I'm released my social position will never again be quite what it was prior to incarceration. Society is so unforgiving. And since life is hard even for those without this status, sheer will and determination hasn't been abandoned. Couple them with the time invested acquiring knowledge and a command of the facts, I won't have to make up for lost time. I will command time. I haven't lost. I have acquired the prerequisites necessary to build things that will stand the test of time. Okay? Just be ready.

Lacino

Dear Andrea,

I've been thinking about your suggestion—submitting an op-ed to the *Wall Street Journal*. Do you have any suggestions for a topic? What do you think about restorative justice?

In the spring of 2013, I had the good fortune to be one of fifteen Michigan prisoners to receive training from the Michigan chapter of the International Institute for Restorative Practices (IIRP). IIRP is a graduate school, based in Bethlehem, Pennsylvania, that envisions a comprehensive framework for practice and theory that expands the restorative paradigm beyond its origins in criminal justice. It offers master's degrees in restorative practices both in education and youth counseling. If I go to school after release, this will more than likely be where I go. Education and youth counseling are passions of mine.

There are many definitions of restorative practices in use, but the concept has its roots in restorative justice. Are you familiar? Restorative justice is a process (to the extent possibly of bringing all stakeholders in a specific offense [crime] together) in order to collectively identify and address harms, needs, and a path to repairing what's been damaged and restoring people. Restorative justice is a way of looking at criminal justice that focuses on repairing people and relationships rather than focusing exclusively on punishment.

Restorative justice did not begin as antiretribution, which it is commonly recognized as today. It began in the 1970s as part of the Victim Offender Mediation Program in Kitchener, Ontario. It was transplanted to Elkhart, Indiana, and then adopted by several Prisoner and Community Together (PACT) program sites. Many participants at the time saw themselves as having been very active in the so-called community-based movement. They were committed to facilitating offenders to take responsibility for their offense by bringing them face to face with those they harmed so they could make things right. They thought it was important for offenders to do more than say they were sorry or feel remorse but for them to learn the full extent of their offense in order to learn what work was required of them to repair and restore people and situations.

Secondarily, but equally important, was involving the community where the harm occurred as opposed to massive institutions like court and prisons taking the human quality out of the process. The question that resonated with me most is when the instructor asked what has really been "broken"—the law, or peoples' lives? By including the community, it gave everyone who suffers when a harm occurs the chance to take part in more substantive ways than filling out a police report and maybe giving testimony if called as a witness. The state is so intrusive that a lot of the times, the victim is only permitted to fill out a police report. They aren't allowed to confront the offender.

It is impossible to restore lives back to their original state after a harm has occurred, but it should be the victim and the community (the primary stakeholders) who have the actual say in what should be done. Have the actual say in what they need to begin the process of making things right. Some victims will be all right with monetary compensation. Others will just want the offender to change their behavior. Some will want the offender to perform community service. Some will want a genuine apology. Some will want the offender to spend time incarcerated and get whatever help they need. Some victims will insist on a combination of actions. And most victims will want to confront the offender(s), tell their story, and hear from the offender.

I know this is rare, but I read a restorative justice narrative where a mother's only son was murdered. After she and the offender shared their stories, as recompense the offender became her surrogate son. Someone told me they would never forgive the murderer of their son, but it worked for them in that situation.

I have learned since my IIRP training that restorative justice has increasingly become an alternative to incarceration by diverse groups working for criminal justice reform, from criminal justice professionals to grassroots organizations. I learned how it has become a reveille for such divergent activities as attempting to meet needs of victims because many victims aren't satisfied with the state dominating the process, reducing probation and parole caseloads, bringing violent offenders and those who survived their violence together in a safe environment for dialogue, mobilizing community members to come together to discuss and take actions regarding crime and delinquency based on interests of the community, and encouraging offenders to take responsibility for their actions.

I learned that empathy and understanding, even moral outrage and condemnation of harm, are not enough to restore victims. The emotional and psychological harm that accompanies the death of a child, the rape of a spouse, the destruction of a business, the theft of a car, among other offenses, does not go away after arrest, a trial, or even a lengthy prison sentence.

One three-day training did not make me a restorative justice expert, but it did convince me that what one victim will accept as adequate reparation another victim will scoff at and that actions taken by some to repair a specific harm can take as many forms as creative minds can devise and agree upon.

The training was really an eye-opener for me. Like a lot of social justice actors that are aware of the current system of the state stepping in (e.g., "The State vs. so and so") when a crime (harm) occurs as if the state has been harmed, or as if the state is the exclusive stakeholder, I had no alternative process in mind but also lacked theory for creating alternatives.

Let me know if you think this is a good topic to write about.

Lacino

Lisa,

I had to put aside what I was doing. I just finished reading your most recent correspondence. Your concern jumped off the pages right into me. Now you got me concerned. Not concerned about your brother, but about the way you are. Concerned about you. It's going to work out. Not just because. But because we are going to work it out. Okay?

I keep writing, asking you to stop saying your brother is crazy. Stop saying how much prison has "fucked him up." This is an abnormal environment. Sometimes a little abnormal is required to make it through. Think of it in these terms: sometimes, when people around you "get ignorant," you get ignorant, right? Not because you are ignorant but because you have to speak and act in a medium they understand, right? In prison "abnormal" is a medium of exchange.

As far as the anxiety your brother is experiencing about release, that's normal. If he asked, "Can I make it on the outside?" that's because he trusts you in ways many incarcerated men and women have no one to trust. You haven't asked that question before because you are out and never been in. You never had a fifteen-year severance in everything he will be expected to pick back up all at once. You have been making it, and eventually, he will too.

That question brackets the next phase of his life. Such a question is demoralizing. That is how I know your brother trusts you. We can identify that as a positive. Many incarcerated men and women think the same thing. Instead of getting it out of their head where others like you and me can contribute, it echoes, turning from anxiety to doubt. Turning from doubt to thinking about "going back in," one of the reasons an appreciable number do return.

Prison claims to be in the business of rehabilitation, resetting our self-regulatory mechanisms so that after release we will maintain the standards of society on our own accord. Not maintain any kind of quality living standards. The standard is accepting the things we so-called cannot change. The outcome has been the undermining of many peoples' abilities to take charge of their life once out.

For fifteen years your brother has had to request permission to execute nearly every detail in his life, like shaving, going to the toilet, telephoning, spending money, mailing letters, and a lot of other minor things. This not only puts him in a submissive and suppliant role unnatural for an adult (can you imagine having to ask permission to do these things?), but it can lead a person to question if they can make it. In fact, when the primary focus is punishment, rehabilitation means "get down or lay down." State-sponsored mob tactics. It's natural for anyone with no freedoms to question if they can exercise them.

What's crazy and fucked up and abnormal is caging people for part or all of their lives. Historically fixed mindsets, entrenched racism, blatant discrimination. If we unpack your brother's question, it is a legitimate question. He may not have questions about making it when released because he questions his ability. He may have questions about making it because once a person is released from prison, life on the outside is a social prison. Having served a prison sentence disqualifies people from anything other than being a hard worker and building a life for someone else. Society's refusal to get out of the way of people leaving prison so they can get on with rebuilding their lives not only reinforces the common perception that we are unworthy of being integrated back into society but that it is impossible to do so.

I may be straying a little off your concern, but only a little. It's important for you to understand that whatever the problem, it's not your brother. The problem is economic and social conditions. The solution is your awareness of this and supporting your brother as he works out of him the doubt the prison put in him.

Your responsibility to your brother is to help build him up. Order some self-esteem books, books on positive reinforcement, books on post-traumatic stress syndrome. You can't just accept everything you read in them, but they can be a starting point. Take what you can use from them. Modify things when necessary. The rest will require patience and understanding. And of course, I'm here for him and you.

Your brother from another mother,

Lacino

Dear Professor, friend of mine,

I thought I explained before that I'm no fan of the government's official crime statistics. Each year the FBI and DOJ release those statistics, the media reports them, politicians argue over who is or will be the toughest going forward, legislators use them to justify billions appropriated for police and prisons, and throughout this entire ritual, their accuracy is never questioned—and it should be.

The many different people and groups that traffic in this deception have glossed over or largely disregarded the issue that what is being measured is not crime per se but what has indisputably been characterized as conventional or "street" crime. Those statistics only measure eight offenses: murder and nonnegligent manslaughter, rape, robbery, aggravated assault, burglary, larceny-theft, motor vehicle theft, and arson. The absence of so-called white-collar crimes (and especially corporate crimes that occur in the world of finance and financial institutions) and political crimes is no mistake.

I have read studies that established that so-called street crime, despite causing far less harm by any credible measure than corporate crime, receives four to five times as much attention. There are so many illegal, unethical, and harmful actions committed by and on behalf of corporations—and occupational crimes committed by individuals, partnerships, and small enterprises—a case can actually be made that the disproportionate attention has traditionally taken the forms of what amounts to an inverse relationship between levels of attention and measures of identifiable harm.

I haven't mentioned state-corporate crimes where crimes are carried out as cooperative ventures between syndicated crime and legitimate businesses, entrepreneurial crimes that some are masquerading as legitimate businesses, or technocrime carried out through the use of computers and other forms of sophisticated technology. The perpetrators of these crimes are culpable of actions with genocidal consequences, which increase the gap between rich and poor, which foster immense ecological and environmental damage, and result in the callous displacement of vast numbers of people here in America and in developing countries. None of this is captured in those FBI and DOJ statistics you mailed.

The particular definitions and conceptions of crime propagated in those statistics not only influence what we think about when we think about crime but also influence in important ways the types of activities law enforcement focuses on. The type of individuals they focus on. And the types of procedures and penalties policy makers adopt. So while judges across the country are throwing the proverbial book at nonviolent cocaine dealers, for example, big pharmaceutical companies are responsible for an opioid "crisis" just as harmful as the 1980s crack cocaine explosion. Big pharmaceutical companies are dealt with through non-criminal regulative procedures. If they are dealt with at all.

There are no police in military gear and battle rams crashing through the front door dragging them out in handcuffs all battered and bloodied to be captured on video by news teams that were tipped off in advance. This is done when a "crime" has occurred, not a "crisis," like the opioid explosion has been defined as.

The simple truth is, crime can be defined in many ways but always seems to focus on people with the least money and who are the most socially vulnerable. Think about all the literature produced on such relatively inconsequential activities as vandalism, petty theft, and marijuana use, but the literature on crimes committed by the state, war crimes, and the violation of human rights is remarkably thin. Those statistics you mailed me cannot begin to express the havoc caused by joblessness and poverty, broken homes, anarchy in communities, both Black and white, the futility in public schools—violations of people and relationships.

I have to end here. Remember, when it comes to statistics, the numbers could be spot-on but flawed and misleading due to the mode of calculation. And therefore, statistics can be both spot-on and useless at the same time.

Your friend,
Lacino

Dear Andrea,

I was born and raised where there are no gray areas. No do-overs. I was born with two strikes, three balls—a full count. No mountaintop experience. Just the valleys and low places where I felt and knew I was vulnerable. Where I either succumbed to misery and constant want or proved that intelligence and sheer determination were more than a match for "them not wanting us to have shit." Sink or swim. If I waited on someone to throw me a life preserver, I probably was going to drown. That is what I was dealing with when I was coming of age in the 1980s.

In 1985, I was eleven. The crack economy. I was drowning in a sea of personal and social changes that were not of my making and for which I had no understanding. I actually thought the rules had been broken and someone had actually thrown me a lifeline. I did not know it was the CIA on the other end and President Ronald Wilson Reagan spitting on the working class and poor. And in true trickle-down fashion—I peddled crack cocaine to people that were losing sight of The Dream. People that were confused.

I am not surprised that a society that once legalized slavery and authorized pursuit of fugitive slaves would create a crack market. American racism toward Blacks was just as much alive then as it had been in 1885. But no one took time to explain this. Not the preacher. Not the teacher. It was unperturbed.

It was no coincidence that so many of us who were trying to have something met up in prison after the CIA had no more use for us. The same CIA counterrevolutionary warfare put down in places like Iran and the Congo around that time was being put down in South Central LA, Detroit, Baltimore—everywhere crack bombs appeared to just explode out of nowhere.

As kids we were all in close interaction with each other: school, someone's basement, in the back of the park where my mother cautioned against hanging out. A change took place in those places. A change took place in our minds. How we were seeing the world. How we were seeing our place in it. We came to tolerate and eventually to evaluate favorably certain deviations for getting to the same place our parents were trying to get. Free of any sense of guilt. A stretched value system.

The differences in range of values from our parents' generation: "fuck being a hard worker just to never have nothing" just to never end up "where we trying to get." We all thought it, even if we couldn't articulate it. I am pretty certain my mother thought it but wouldn't articulate it. Within that range a lot of desperate activity occurred, primarily as an adaptive rather than as a cultural response. This is where context matters, where comparative presentation matters. I seriously doubt that others who were not in danger of drowning were thinking any differently—about having things. Granted there were differences in means. But the CIA wasn't on the other end of their line.

Today I still don't have things. I want things. I just haven't had the opportunity to put my skill set in rotation. Of course prison has been the culprit. But it shouldn't be much longer. The dynamics won't be as predictable. I want freedom. My mentor, Chokwe Lumumba, told me to "free the land." I want real justice. Not that "shoot me in the back for looking suspicious sitting in my car, send me 455 miles away from my family and friends to a maximum security prison"-style justice. I want power. Without power I am forced to use cunning, deception, guile. Exhausting. Certainly others have used these arts to survive, but that's because they did not have the things I want. The things I am determined to have—in this world, not the next.

I started late. It's getting late. I have to prepare this to be mailed. Keep asking questions. I will keep trying to answer them. In the process I hope you come to see me as I really am.

Lacino

"For the kind of sustainable peace to be achieved that makes the restoration of victims possible, it is crucial for perpetrators to be incorporated into the emerging new society."

—United Nations New Agenda for the
Development of Africa, 1990[8]

Dear Rhonda,

I was outside today for about thirty minutes. It was frigid noontime in Baraga, "Mississippi." The racism here is so out in the open it's as if Baraga is a small town in 1950s Mississippi, not 2007 Michigan. The brisk winter wind was whistling through the yard with nothing to break it up or shield us from it. The yard is just an open area where we walk in circles like a hamster on a wheel. Insane, isn't it? I had to come in, leaving thirty minutes of yard time on the clock.

When I entered the housing unit, several guards were standing around the control panel. I have to pass it on my way to the cell. They were laughing about the line of work they are in: "people work." They all seemed to look in my direction at the same time, then laughed harder. Once back in the cell, I sat down and thought about what they were saying, and more important, what it meant.

Prisons are presented to the public as rational institutions designed as effective machines for "fixing people." When in reality they are merely storage dumps. I'm in-cell twenty-three hours a day. When I do come out, it's to walk in circles around an empty field about the size of your front yard. The contradiction between what the prison does and what people employed by the prison say it does is worlds apart. People work?

I know that they didn't come up with that term. The seven of them together couldn't think their way out of a parking lot. But they meant something by it. And by the way their bodies shook and jiggled when they laughed, it wasn't good. Are we supposed to be some kind of material, some kind of inanimate object to be hammered on, stretched out, bent in different shapes? Perhaps this is why prison rules are used as a blunt instrument. Why I don't have rights in prison. Why a judge recently ruled that human standards in the prison setting are unnecessary standards.

There are some assignments prison guards prefer to work over others, such as segregation. In segregation we get less, expect less, so guards do less. There are fewer time-consuming requests than in other parts of the prison. Guards prefer to do absolutely nothing at all.

The full meaning of people work has something to do with creating and sustaining a particular kind of tension between the world out there and the world in here and using that tension as strategic leverage in managing us. This is what guards do. In the world out there, before we entered prison, our personal organization was part of a wider framework lodged in experiences that allowed for a set of defensive maneuvers for coping with conflicts, exercised at our own discretion. They have one of those sociological-sounding names for eradicating this out of us: disculturation. An un-training that is supposed to render us incapable of putting up a fight, the way we did prior to incarceration. In a curious way, all that bullshit we were doing prior to prison was proof that we still had sufficient strength to rebel and had not yet given in to defeat.

A guard's work isn't to come up with disculturation schemes. If it was, they would fail miserably. I meant it, they cannot think their way out of a parking lot. But when they enforce prison policies and rules, which is what they are paid to do, disculturation is accomplished. It's really not the guards; it's the policies and rules. Guards can be changed out like tires and it will not affect the efficiency of the prison. This is why when we challenge what an individual guard does, they fall back on the line, "I'm just enforcing the rules." We might not like what they are doing, but that's exactly what they are doing. If guards could think independently of the prison, or could find work elsewhere, they would be of no use to the prison.

Because prisons are merely storage dumps, and the neighborhood will not have substantially changed when we are released, all defensive maneuvers exercised at our own discretion, any strength to rebel, signs that we haven't yet given into defeat, have to be rooted out of us—people work.

At least since the nineteenth century, the people who traffic in this particular brand of misery have been cognizant of the paradigmatic psychiatric disturbances correlated with incarceration (e.g., paranoia, severe confusion, intense agitation, self-directed violence). This is what they were uncontrollably laughing at—imposing significant psychological pain. Impairing our capacity to defend ourselves. I know what I'm sharing with you is correct, but I want you to research this so you know. So you know the importance of aligning your interests with mine. I'm thirteen years in, but not out of the fight. I never will be, but that doesn't mean I don't need you in it with me.

Lacino D. Hamilton

Carl,

I understand you may feel a responsibility to contradict and challenge misinformation and stereotypic beliefs—I feel that responsibility, too. However, get it out of your head that you can make someone learn something, because you can't. You need to remember, or learn, that the decision to embrace new information and shed beliefs belongs to the person or people you are in dialogue with, not you. What you can do is expose individuals or groups, depending on the setting, to information they may otherwise not come in contact with, or haven't up until this point, and offer new perspectives that augment or challenge current worldviews, but you cannot force awareness on anyone.

The same way you bring an array of assumptions and implicit worldviews that have been affirmed in your everyday interactions with family, peers, and the larger society, so do they. Those assumptions and worldviews are part of their identity, a part of what helps them feel centered. Shoving a book in someone's face or giving them your best spiel doesn't just obliterate what makes them feel centered. Actually, just the opposite is likely to occur. The natural reaction when someone is challenged is for them to vigorously defend against discordant information or experiences presented to them. So you just have to be patient with people, and consistent.

You also have to get it out of your head that people develop in a linear fashion, or on some predictable timeline. This is one of the major flaws in the US school system (i.e., that everyone should develop at the same pace and at the same time). What one person may grasp the first time may take another person several times, or several dozen times, which doesn't signify some kind of cognitive maldevelopment. Of course you should push people. But how hard is an art, not a science. And all of us aren't artists.

Furthermore, everyone does not learn the same way. It's common for people that take on some kind of teaching role to force upon those they are in dialogue with the model of learning that works for them, when learning doesn't work like that. You may be a read-and-grasp type person, others may be more experimental and interactively oriented. You may have a great memory, while others, like me, may be all short term. Some people you will have to be more hands on with, some people work great independently. All you can really do is offer a broad framework for creating supportive conditions in which people can engage new ideas and perspectives.

I would like to continue this, but I am pressed for time. I will end by asking, have you ever heard the adage that "the teacher must be taught?" I think it would aid you greatly to invest time in studying different pedagogical models. What you criticize in others could be your own shortcomings, not theirs.

Lacino

Dear Professor James A.,

Please forgive me for taking so long to respond. I'm usually prompt with the turnaround. Anyone who takes time out of their day to add some much-needed variety to my boring life I would never purposely keep waiting. Correspondence is medicine in print form, a hook and ladder, an extravaganza. (Told you my life is boring.)

I was waiting until after my attorneys visited. That way I could give all my attention to your questions. But every time I look over and see your letter, it bothers me. So I would appreciate if you accepted the following as a point of departure. By the time you respond, my attorneys should have come and gone. There will be nothing to distract from your very important inquiries.

Okay, how we approach prison abolition, the problems we identify as needing remedy, the solutions we entertain as viable, and the methods we choose as appropriate for reaching those solutions are all theoretical as well as practical questions. Articulating the theoretical source of our approaches to prison abolition serves important purposes. For example:

1. The prison abolition movement represents the moral consciousness of America and therefore naturally belongs in the forefront of the movement for economic and social justice.

2. Prison abolition is unachievable under the present organization of American society, and therefore prison abolition must be fought for as part of a larger effort to remake American society, as a whole.

3. Prison systems across the country are affected by a similar array of social, political, and economic forces, but there is tremendous variation in the way that these forces operate in "local" contexts that feature unique political structures, populations, and histories. Much of the variation is neglected or obscured in favor of broad trends that have affected many communities throughout the country.

4. Although individuals do play a part, American policies do not stem from personal whims but from the necessities of the American socioeconomic system and its political manifestations. Prison abolition must put maximum pressure on those systems and manifestations.

We begin here in an effort to develop clear ways to define, analyze, and understand how imprisonment operates at individual, cultural, and institutional levels, historically as well as in the present. We also begin here in our effort to act more effectively against oppressive circumstances as they arise in our abolition. Any strategy for abolishing prison must be based on theory shaped by what and how we do it. Not fantasies.

This will allow us to think clearly about our intentions and the means we use to actualize them. It provides a framework for making choices about what we do and how, and for distinguishing among different approaches. At its best it also provides a framework for questioning and challenging what we do and how we do it as we encounter inevitable problems of co-optation, resistance, insufficient knowledge, and changing social conditions.

What we do and how we do it should allow us to anticipate these state reactions in advance of them and have "responses" that turn into offense and put the state on its heels, not us. Ideally we keep coming back to and refining what we do and how we do it as we discuss, reflect, and continually further our abolition.

We must remain cognizant of our position as historical subjects and cognizant of the potential to learn from the past as we remain open to creating new approaches to meet conditions in more effective and imaginative ways. I'm looking to hoist and plant a flag. Martyrs are last options. Especially considering there are so few of us at this present moment.

Sounds kind of clinical, I know, but the prison movement is at an impasse precisely because it lacks a functional theory (i.e., brain) able to confront and deal perceptively with American realities on a level that social conditions demand. For this reason all those who would refer to themselves as any variation of prison abolitionist must know their politics and keep them in the forefront of their actions.

This is where we will begin, but it is not where we will end. Push. Push. Push. Push people forward toward greater commitments. Commitments that require greater levels of humanity, determination, and courage. If you catch my drift. And if the results are wanting, change positions. Pull. Pull. Pull. Pull people into greater levels of commitments.

I have to bring this to a close. Look forward to your response.

Rebuilding to win,
Lacino

Morning, Rhonda,

Have you ever heard the phrase, "I'm not a doctor but I play one on television"? Well prison staff aren't doctors, but they often play the role of one in real life, diagnosing assumed problems of prisoners. And if that doesn't go too far living out fantasies, they prescribe remedies also. It would be just a subpar display of talent if this role playing wasn't marked with injurious consequences affecting both the mind and body, but it does.

"Do you know what your problem is, Hamilton?" A question I hear several times per day. "What's that?" Staff need me to come back with "What's that?" so they can deliver the punch line. Mind you, it's 6:04 in the morning. The guard who's only been on shift four minutes is already in full character (clown). It's as if he was up the entire night rehearsing this. And since I'm up reading every morning when he walks by, I'm just the unlucky prisoner drafted into the charade.

"See, your problem is…" and it really depends on exactly what I'm doing. If I'm reading, my problem is I think I can read. If I'm writing, my problem is I think I can write. If I have law books sprawled across what masquerades as a mattress, my problem is I still think somebody cares about me not getting a fair trial. This particular guard looked the case up on the internet. Most of the time my problem is, "You think you're smart." Of all the so-called problems a prisoner can have, prison staff respond to "thinking you're smart" as if it is a deadly virus.

It doesn't end there. Not just this guard, but there is something about the prison that causes staff to pointedly appoint themselves as specialists in the knowledge of punishment. No matter what the so-called problem, the prescription is the use of punishment as a means of inducing behavior change. Never mind that there are volumes of accounts that detail how punishment is inherently suspect ethically and creates inherent risk of harm.

"What you need, Hamilton," here comes the prescription, "is some solitary confinement time"; "you need some hard labor in your life"; "all those books should be taken from you." I'm sitting here reading or writing or going over the case, which this staff views as a problem. And the prescription is total isolation, physical and emotional taxing labor, "and/ or" intellectual deprivation. Make that make sense.

An important part of management theory in prison is the belief that if prisoners can be made to show extreme deference to staff immediately upon arrival to prison, or immediately upon arrival after transfer to a different prison, or transfer to a different part of the prison, we will thereafter be manageable. If we submit to initial demands (the number-one rule in prison is follow *all* rules given by *all* staff), our resistance or spirit is somehow broken. A broken spirit is the goal of management theory.

When I first began studying management theory, particularly in the prison setting, I didn't want to believe what I was understanding. Management theory doesn't just come out and say the goal is to break our spirit. At least it doesn't in popular textbooks. I'm certain there are white papers somewhere that do. But as I began going behind the meaning of words and witnessed management theory in action, I saw how things you and I (or any other rational person) would never think of as problems are actually problems in prison. And the prescription is some form of punishment.

The windows in the cell block are covered. There is a small area at the bottom from which the sky can be seen. If a staff member walks by and sees one of us trying to look out and sees the night sky, "the problem is you think there is something out there for you." And it's almost as if they have a prescription handbook. "What you need is to sit down on that bunk or I can move you to a cell where you can't see anything but chipped paint." What?

Looking at the night sky is interpreted as microresistance, the capacity to conceive of a world beyond prison. And that is a problem. It's proof that there is life still inside of us and that makes the prison's management of us more difficult.

I would like to add a final point before I get back to doing what I was doing. I wanted to get this out of my head so it doesn't distract me any more than it has. The more I understand the less likely anger and frustration will express itself in harmful ways. But this is why education was abolished in prison—it was a problem. At least to prison staff.

Education is the antithesis of management theory. It's easier to manage an uninformed population than one that is. It's nearly impossible to break the spirit of knowledgeable people, of people that are cognizant of what's going on because when one is aware, one tends to act, and act accordingly. Prison staff do not want prisoners possessing knowledge and critical thinking skills. They strengthen the spirit. And with them we will naturally do what any other group would do with them if under attack—fight.

I hope the rest of your day is a million times better than mine. I have a feeling prison staff will never stop trying to punish me until they believe my spirit is broken. Then they can hold me up as a trophy of some sort. You said a few years back I was a trophy, but this isn't what you had in mind.

Bloody but not broken,
Lacino Darnell Hamilton

Dear Rhonda,

Yes, filing a lawsuit did cross my mind. The same way a meteor crosses the sky: there one second, gone the next. Courts have struck some kind of "gentleman's" agreement with prisons to let them do just about anything to us short of murder. And often they turn a blind eye to that also. Filing a lawsuit can be a more demoralizing judicial experience than the one leading to our incarceration.

In the last couple decades, when prisoners file lawsuits, the courts have given us the middle finger. Trimming our access to the court. Abolishing due process protections. Falling silent when it comes to First Amendment rights. I call judges that preside over lawsuits filed by prisoners "pirates." You know how pirates wear a patch over one eye? Seeing and not seeing at the same time? Judges are biased and prejudiced against us. That's the patched eye. With the eye they can see out of, they emphasize the importance of "deference" to the judgment of prison officials.

American prisons are filled disproportionately with people of color. Judges are mostly white, middle-class, middle-aged (and older), usually male members of the establishment who have more in common with people who run prisons than prisoners. Even judges who are women, members of minority groups, or younger are pirates too. This does not mean pirates cannot or will not be fair, but more often than not, they won't. They will not assume prison guards falsify disciplinary reports to cover up their own misbehavior, but they do.

Pirates, like many people in the general society, believe that prison conditions that amount to cruel and unusual punishment are part of the penalty that incarcerated men and women pay when convicted. For example, the US Supreme Court has consistently ruled that prolonged idleness and deprivation from all human contact does not deny basic human needs of companionship and meaningful activity. I guarantee they don't want to be locked in a cell by themselves for years.

I can send you a court case to read where a pirate recently ruled that "the sadistic use of force, even when it inflicts pain or injury, is justified when prison officials act in good faith." Can someone act sadistically and act in good faith at the same time? That's why I call them pirates: seeing and not seeing.

An officer continuously banged and kicked on Mr. Johnson's cell door. Threw food trays through the slot so hard the top came off. Made aggravating remarks, insulted him about his hair length (kept calling him a girl), growled and snarled through the cell window and smeared it so he couldn't see out. The guard repeatedly called him a nigger and jerked and pulled him unnecessarily hard when he escorted him from his cell. The guard demonstrated shameful and utterly unprofessional behavior. But when Mr. Johnson filed a lawsuit, a pirate ruled that the guard's behavior was insufficient to establish an Eighth Amendment violation.

A pirate in a different court ruled that placement in a concrete cell with no heat, no clothing, no mattress, no blankets or any other bedding, no prescription eyeglasses, no out-of-cell exercise, no utensils, no ventilation, no hot water, and no toilet paper for sixty days was not a significant departure from the "healthy habilitative environment" the prison is required to provide us.

Last year a group of prisoners who have been routinely subjected to violence, extortion, and rape by guards, the same guards who prevented them from seeking safekeeping or protective custody, who were promoted to supervisors three weeks after the lawsuit was filed, were ruled against, and the pirate who ruled that stated the determining factor of why he sided with the guards was "the short length of time prisoners were subjected to the unpleasant conditions." Violence, extortion, and rape against prisoners is acceptable as long as the duration is brief?

In rare occasions the courts have found disciplinary punishment disproportionate to the disciplinary offense. However, most courts rule that if punishment is not specifically imposed as part of our sentence, it is not really punishment unless the prison staff imposing it "possesses a sufficiently culpable state of mind." That had to be written to confuse. When a clarification was requested, the pirate topped herself and wrote, "This applies to security policies that are developed over time with ample opportunity for reflection." Upon further request for clarification, the court dismissed the lawsuit in its entirety under the "frivolousness clause."

None of us are lawyers. It takes a lot of research and effort to write a lawsuit—just to have it summarily dismissed. And that's on top of the fact that the Prison Litigation Reform Act (PLRA) makes it more difficult for us to pursue legal claims. The PLRA requires us to pay $350 to file a lawsuit (appeals cost an additional $450). It requires indigent prisoners, unlike other indigent litigants, to pay fees in installments. That means if a friend or family member sends us money, the courts take it until they get theirs. And under some circumstances, being indigent bars us from filing.

These are just a few examples of why filing lawsuits against prisons and their employees isn't a viable form of redress. If we file it really isn't to win. It's really about documenting and creating a record of abuses. Perhaps as those documents and records grow, prisoner advocacy groups will come to realize there is an immediacy attached to all of this. Perhaps more of the public will get involved. Outside of that we're just going to have to rock out on this end.

All ten toes ...
Lacino

Dear Professor Shari,

In the past two weeks, five of the books you mailed were rejected. There is no penological interest for this. It's censorship, plain and simple. The prison operates under the theory that it is easier to control an ignorant population than one that is informed, so we are deprived of as much information as the prison can get away with. This started long before I got here.

In the 1960s and 1970s, larger numbers of Michigan prisoners were politicized. Books played a major role. People in here began reading in ways they weren't prior to being locked up, and through academic research, writing, and speaking, prisoners were learning how to be critical with information, analyze data, and formulate complex ideas. Most of all they were learning to enjoy the intellectual adventure enough to be able to do it easily and often.

It was a unique and extraordinary time in the history of self-education in Michigan prisons. A time when events were happening at such a rapid and desperate pace in the larger society that it would have been impossible for prisoners to be completely left out. A time that promoted dialogue, debate, and dialectical exchange. An atmosphere that influenced independent and radical thinking, which created a host of problems that MDOC was not equipped at the time to handle.

In order for prison officials to more tightly control our lives, reduce us to active accomplices and passive recipients of a daily round of life alien to us, officials began to stop the free flow of information into prison. Information is power. The more one knows about something, or the more one knows period, the more power they have to understand themselves and others and how to be more effective.

The right information feeds the idea that a nearly hopeless situation like prison can be changed. I know this from reading authors like George L. Jackson and Mumia Abu Jamal. Those of us who are harmed the least by this experience are usually those who develop analysis of power in social structures. They tend not to personalize this experience. They do not look at a harmful experience and spend all their time thinking about what is wrong with them. Instead, they ask what is wrong with the situation.

What the MDOC began to do in the 1980s and 1990s was to systematically restrict access to a broad range of topics and authors that were likely to influence critical thinking or were a product of critical thinking. Prison officials do not want us thinking about prison in critical ways. Therefore less and less information is allowed in. Prison officials are literally and figuratively the gatekeepers.

I do not think books have ever just been about fighting back boredom or killing time for men and women in prison. Reading has always been an important means of discovery, feeding imagination, thinking about more than following rules, and preparing for release. The more one knows, the more they can do. Information is arguably the most powerful tool available to us inside these places. It is through the control of information that prison officials maintain power. Essentially it is a political struggle. Something that groups who dominate other groups have understood for centuries.

Of course it would be an oversimplification to completely attribute the restriction of information into prison to the Machiavellian designs to prison officials. Seventy percent of people enter prison without a GED or high school diploma. Fifty-five percent have an elementary education or less. Acquiring information would be a challenge even if prison officials were not actively trying to stop us. But this is the very reason why prison officials should promote numerous and creative ways to become more informed.

There will always be a minority of prisoners who are super determined to find ways to self-educate, but censorship in prison is so effective that self-educated and critically thinking prisoners are becoming a rarity, making all that talk about prisons being a poor person's university a myth. Worst of all, though, is that when people are released from prison, that censorship will be the most pronounced. It is going to be virtually impossible to keep up after years of being held down and back.

I wonder, would the public be outraged if they knew this was happening, in their name? Do not stop sending information. Some of that you send makes it through the censors, and I always make the best of it.

Your friend,
Lacino

Dear Lisa,

You want to know why I write so much about prison? My question to you is, why aren't others writing more? Most of the people who live in America associate extremist ideology with Arabs, socialist countries, or cultures different from America's in general. Few people associate extremist ideology with locking people up. I am trying to change that.

Prison has become so deeply embedded within the culture and collective psyche that most people accept prison as something natural, when it is not. Prison has become the solution to nearly every problem but solves none. All sorts of ideological, political, social, and psychological barriers insert themselves into the criminal justice process. Call it what you will, but caging people is extreme. Micromanaging peoples' lives down to feeding time, bathroom time, shower time, and yard time resembles how animals are managed.

Prison is the epitome of tyrannical decision-making. The epitome of isolation and marginalization. The epitome of censorship and silence. The epitome of structural violence. The epitome of hypocrisy. Everything that is supposedly frowned on when dictators and autocrats inflict it on the people in their countries is all right to do to people in American prisons. I just keep thinking that the average person does not know what really goes on in these places, so people have to write and speak out at every available opportunity. When opportunities do not exist, we have to get creative and manufacture them.

Besides, if I do not write, who will? What I am living with here does not allow me to wait until others fully wake up to the serious harm prisons cause. People who are concerned with America's use of prison are basically concerned with how much they are in use, not with what that use actually means. It is not enough to simply limit how many people are tortured in this way. The goal, in my opinion, has to be finding alternatives to sending people to prison.

I have had people tell me this sounds insane, but that is only because they think I am talking about finding alternatives to prison while keeping everything else in our society the same—that will not work. In order to envision a world, for example, without prisons, we have to envision a totally different world. How we relate to ourselves, others, the environment, and what we consider the community all have to be different. Since prisons are extreme, they require extreme responses and challenges. That is why I write so much about prison.

Lacino

Mom & Dad,

Just one time I would like to read a letter from you without experiencing a migraine afterward. There is no way you can really believe what you wrote: God put me here for a reason. Really? I have never believed in fairy tales. Not even as a child. So please never write me anything remotely close to that again.

You do not have to lie to me. It does not help me or the development of the bridge I am trying to build to meet you two somewhere in the middle—between your acceptance of a life plagued by constant setbacks and disappointments and the life that I am building where hard work and sacrifice will actually benefit us. God did not put me here. Lying ass detective James Fleming and serial witness Oliver Cowan put me here. I know who my enemies are—do you?

I sometimes think that men invented the God concept so that they could be intellectually lazy, just like you. So that they did not have to take responsibility for the things happening around them. When has closing one's eyes, wishing a problem away, then reopening one's eyes ever eliminated a problem? It never has.

The great Zulu warrior Shaka taught that that was the kind of insanity that allowed Afrika to be stolen from our ancestors. He said that when the missionaries came to Afrika, our ancestors had the land and they had the bibles. They taught our ancestors how to pray with their eyes closed. When they reopened their eyes, the missionaries had the land, and our ancestors had the bibles.

Shaka also taught that in order to solve a problem, one must go to the heart of it. A problem clearly envisaged, a point succinctly made, holds the elements of the solution in itself. He taught that every solution must be susceptible to mathematical expression. And that every problem is the result of movement and rhythms that give it form and character. I do not have to close my eyes and talk to myself to know I got a raw deal. That police and prosecutors made me a criminal, not my actions.

God has not made our lives a living hell. People greedy for profit have. The same people who made ghettos, who reengineered the chemical components of cocaine and came up with crack, and who eliminated jobs and underfunded schools knew in advance that people affected by these would resort to living by wit, which is outlawed if Uncle Sam isn't getting a cut. Shame on you for not giving Ford, Chrysler, Walmart, Exxon, Nestle, Firestone, Colgate, Blackwater, Compuware, Dole, and the rest of the greedy capitalists credit for creating the dull reality in which we live. For not thanking them for creating the conditions that made you and me surplus, and therefore expendable.

Mom, Dad, never look for yourself in the world. That would be to project your illusions. If God is not in you, you will find God nowhere. But if God is in you, you will find God everywhere. Learn to know the world in yourself, like I have. Do you follow? You have the power to do more than play victim. But first you must believe in yourself, and people like me.

Mom, Dad, you underestimate me. I am a representation of what social justice and human rights agents are building: noble, disciplined, heroic, intrepid, audacious, resourceful, indomitable. I am all the things you pray for but will not fight for. Make that make sense. You'd rather advise me to close my eyes and wish than contribute to getting me free. I wonder what Shaka would have said about that?

Lacino Darnell H.

Dear Maya,[*]

Most people are aware that being incarcerated is not the best of all possible lives, but few understand the human costs. Few understand that most people who leave these places do so traumatized. And when many people experience similar personal troubles, these troubles cannot be defined as personal in nature, though they have deeply personal consequences. The procedures and policies that govern the operation of prisons constitute a social-structural problem ...

It is a tragedy of the first magnitude that millions of people have been reduced to dependence on guards for the most basic services, isolated from the rest of the world's population, confined to a fixed habitat, coerced to work for little or no compensation, and subjected to a prison culture that breeds a profound sense of depression, a personal worthlessness and despair, all in the name of justice. Making invisible a growing underclass. Expelling self-determination, exacerbating weaknesses, exhausting strength, and suppressing experience of intelligence in an aim to produce a robot-like mass that will blindly follow the rules of prison—even when they run counter to our safety and best interests.

When we enter prison, we are immediately stripped of the conditions and materials that make individual identity possible. In the language of penologists, a series of abasements, degradations, humiliations, and profanations of self occur. Everyone goes to bed and wakes at the same time, everyone wears the same prison-issued uniform, everyone eats the same tasteless food, everyone receives the same paucity of information, and everyone is punished, even when it is just an individual or small group that broke the rules. With many of our previous bases for self-identification gone, a serious curtailment happens.

Prison admission policies might better be called trimming or programming because when we enter, attempts are made to shape and code

---

[*] Maya Schenwar, editor of *Truthout*, which published some of Lacino's essays.

us into an object that can be fed into the administrative machinery of the prison. To be worked on smoothly by routine operations. And because all phases of the day's activities are tightly scheduled, there is a special need for guards to obtain our cooperation. I am talking about extreme deference. When there isn't, punishment is swift, grotesque, and demoralizing to say the least.

Many people have been conditioned by popular culture and formal institutions to believe prison should not be a picnic and wonder what I expect the ordeal of incarceration to be like when I speak out against the treatment here. We are expected to fully prostrate in order to mitigate punishment, required to beg for little things like toiletries, a drink of water, or permission to speak or sit down. And there is no guarantee the permission will be granted. Instead, it is likely we will be questioned at length, denied, teased, or simply ignored. We must reorganize our lives around learning to win the favor of guards. This usually consists of becoming an informant, a reorganization that promotes an extremely demeaning brand of individualism.

It is remarkable with all the harm that prison inflicts that when cost is brought into the discussion, it's monetary—the human cost is not the subject. I really believe people just do not know. I mean they know prison is no place they would ever want to live, but they do not know to what degree our lives are micromanaged and what it takes for guards to do so efficiently. It's depressing is what it is. Just depressing. I am going to write an essay about this and get it to you soon. But promise me that next time someone around you mentions the cost of incarcerating people, convey to them the human cost of incarcerating people.

Take care,
Lacino

IV

Dear Professor James A.,

I do not have the time to sit here and run down the complete history of the Civil Rights Movement. Even with the luxury of hindsight, what I think about the boycotts, marches, pleading, praying, groveling, and occasional threatening to tear some white person's head off would easily fill up a few notepads. What I will say, and what I hope is of some use to you, is that it was done so smoothly, it had to be a plan.

The struggle to bring down Jim Crow and segregation was unpredictable as long as it remained in the community. There, at any time, it could spill over into the streets, where the outcome would be determined by how long people stayed there, and how far they were willing to go. Therefore, from the government's perspective, two things had to happen: (1) the struggle needed official spokespeople recognized by the masses and the government; and (2) the struggle had to move out of the community, out of the streets, and into the courts.

Once there were people who appeared to speak for everyone (I don't think middle-class Blacks and liberal whites really accepted King until 1964 when he received the Nobel Peace Prize) and the battleground became legal arguments and precedents, the government could control the outcome. It's like that today when people protest and riot in the streets. The government can only attempt to control the masses through military weapons and tactics, which do not work. It isn't until so-called official spokespeople call for an official investigation or a grand jury that protesters and rioters are sidelined. That is the history of the Civil Rights Movement in a nutshell.

We are now five decades removed from that period. Two generations have reached adulthood. The true measurement of the successes and failures of *Brown v. Board of Education*, the sit-in movement, Freedom Summer, the March on Washington, Bloody Sunday, the Voting Rights Act, and so on can now be assessed. Assessment does not lie with the generation of adults who lived through those sacrifices and events. The rest is whether the children and grandchildren of the civil rights era have achieved the promises of the period. The short answer is, we haven't.

Despite the high hopes of the times, the past two generations of Blacks have made virtually no advancement in quality of education, residential desegregation, the consequences of persistent exposure to the nation's poorest neighborhoods, ending police violence, state surveillance, disproportionate representation—in nearly every statistic no one wants that part of the Black demographic to lead. Millions of Black people live in remarkably similar environments to fifty years ago.

Now, of course, there are some exceptions. Mostly athletes, musicians, actors, and other entertainers. The progress they represent is symbolic. Most whites and a lot of Blacks rely on symbols to support their belief that Black people have come a long way since the civil rights era. In their view we not only can sit wherever we want on filthy public transportation, spend our money with people who openly show disdain for us, choose between the lesser of the two evils, but there is a holiday for King. All symbols. None of this has given us the power to define reality and have others adhere to it.

We celebrate basketball players and reality TV stars "making it" while there are more Black men in prison than in college, more Black people out of work now than at any time since slavery. The country does nothing about the violence in Chicago neighborhoods that reflect the violence in Chicago housing, education, and employment practices. We celebrate Jay Z and Beyoncé, Lebron and Dr. Dre's riches, which are not connected to oil, steel, fiber optics, military-grade weapons or any other resource of [inter]national importance. They are all symbols that will not cost white supremacy much and at the same time will help keep Blacks pacified.

The best thing we can do as far as evaluating the Civil Rights Movement's successes and failures is to get beyond the symbols of advancement, get beyond the bourgeoise Black folks with all their degrees and fancy gadgets who still do not understand what we ordinary Blacks have known for a very long time: popular depictions of civil rights romanticize America's civil rights years as an era in which the country came together, while it also indicts today's Blacks for failing to take advantage of the sacrifices made during that period. Popular depictions gloss over the subtler complexities of white supremacy's enduring legacy. This is an uncomfortable reality for a lot of people, but reality, nonetheless.

My friend, the Civil Rights Movement remains one of the most misunderstood social movements. It is going to take a lot of microdissecting to understand why after so much has changed, so much remains the same. A lot.

Lacino

Dear Professor James A.,

It was great receiving a letter from you. Thank you for asking how I have been doing. I've been keeping it pushing. Years ago that question used to infuriate me. I would respond with something like, "I'm doing fifty-two to eighty years." Just to keep it front and center. Another way of saying I'm under a lot of pressure. That I need help.

Your advice about seeking medical care from the prison: these veterinarians and witch doctors would let me die first. I shouldn't say that. Comparing the people here that work in health care to veterinarians and witch doctors is an insult to the latter two. I'd probably receive better care from a veterinarian or witch doctor.

Since we cannot obtain our own medical services, the Constitution requires the prison to provide us with "reasonably adequate" medical care. And there goes the flaw and potential to neglect our health right there. Who decides what is reasonably adequate and what isn't? Those that speak legalese say reasonably adequate medical care "requires treatment by qualified medical personnel who provide services that are of quality acceptable when measured by prudent professional standards in the community, tailored in our particular needs, and that are based on medical considerations."[1] Don't you just like the way they put words together? Saying a lot and saying nothing at the same time.

Before I unpack that, whatever private insurance company contracted to run the MDOC medical services decides what is and what isn't reasonably adequate. What is and isn't going to cost them money. Nurses and doctors always have to "check first" with the health care provider, a.k.a. the insurance company. And it's far time we expand our definition of private prisons. Usually we think of private prisons as a company that operates a prison for profit. But here in Michigan the state still operates the prison but has "contracted out" (i.e., privatized) many of the essential services (e.g., health services, food services, telephone services, prison industries, and commissary). Instead of one company privatizing and operating Michigan prisons for profit, many companies operate for profit.

But let's look closer at this public relations–crafted double talk. I know what usually comes to mind when we hear terms like "qualified medical personnel," but scratch that. It's been discovered (and kept quiet) that medical staff on at least six or seven occasions has consisted of unlicensed doctors, untrained prisoners, and an untrained pharmacist. It's happened out there where you are—people masquerading as medical professionals. So don't think it doesn't happen in prison.

Actually it would be much easier to impersonate a nurse or doctor in here because it doesn't require professional training or a license to tell us "No," "We'll get back to you," or the one that borders on ridicule in my opinion, "Drink more water." We can crawl into the medical building with a bone sticking out of our back and the person in the white coat who may or may not be a doctor or nurse will tell us, "Drink more water." And this doesn't even account for medical personnel who've been run out of another state or public practice (i.e., not qualified) but work in prison.

"Quality acceptable" is highly subjective. Quality acceptable is sort of like beauty—in the eye of the beholder. But acceptable to who? We don't have a choice but to accept because there are no options, despite the rhetoric we hear about choice being the best business model. And I wouldn't call making decisions about medical priorities from our written complaints without an examination or inadequately trained guards using their own judgment about the seriousness of an injury or not testing for disease to be acceptable quality.

Several years ago I read in the newspaper that as many as eighteen thousand Michigan prisoners may have hepatitis. There are a number of different types of hepatitis. Hepatitis C is the variety that is most widespread in the prison population, a viral infection that causes liver disease, which in some cases may progress to cirrhosis (serious scarring of the liver), which may be fatal.

It may be many years after infection before the disease is advanced enough to make a person feel sick, though some people experience symptoms such as appetite loss, fatigue, nausea and vomiting, vague stomach pain, and jaundice (a yellowing of the skin and whites of the eyes) within two weeks to six months after infection. The newspaper article detailed how the MDOC doesn't test for hepatitis C despite estimates that maybe a third of the prisoner population is infected.

Hepatitis C is diagnosed by a simple blood test. And testing is recommended for anyone at risk for infection. Of course, it is difficult to obtain treatment because it's difficult to obtain tests. Possibly because some of the treatments are expensive.

As far as health care being "measured by 'prudent' professional standards in the community," what community? The prison community? The larger community in general? Poor communities? Wealthy and affluent communities? What's prudent and professional standards for the prison community definitely isn't what's prudent and professional say, for example, the director of the MDOC's community or the governor's community. Prison rarely provides the complete range of necessary medical service. Sucks to be a prisoner because if the insurance company doesn't permit prison doctors and nurses to give us aspirin, they definitely aren't going to pay an outside hospital or specialist to provide us treatment at market prices.

And as to the last part, "tailored to our particular needs that are based on medical consideration," it's vague enough to graft onto it a thousand different meanings. Usually, though, "particular needs" and "medical considerations" are justified as a so-called differences of opinion. Two weeks ago I was denied treatment for a cold because the dude in the white coat told me, "Research shows there is nothing that can be done for a cold." When I shot back that the cold industry is a multibillion-dollar industry with libraries full of research that says just the opposite, he laughed, said "I stand corrected," and hurried me out the office—with the proverbial bone sticking out my back.

And don't get me started on mental health care. Complaints about depression and feelings of suicide are so common, the people in the white coats don't even pay it any attention. At least not until a prisoner has attempted to hang themselves or cut their wrist, which has happened more and more frequently over the last ten years. And the response has simply been to immobilize them with medication. I'm no doctor, but this appears to erode self-esteem and induce apathy, fear, and feelings of differentness.

An adequate mental health care system begins with a systematic program for continuous screening and evaluating, to identify those of us in need of mental health care, not a psychotropic drug pusher. A mental health care system that only provides services to those that self-report, which is what's going on in here, is not a mental health care system. Basically we are required to self-diagnose mental health care needs. Make that make sense.

My point is we have to *get me free*. I need surgery, and the prison couldn't care less. Prison and medical care spoken in the same sentence is grammatically incorrect. Oxymoronic. Verbal malpractice. It's too much money involved for the prison to correct itself. We're going to have to correct things ourselves.

Once again, it was great hearing from you,
Lacino

Dear MI-CURE,[*]

It seems like forever since I last sent correspondence. It's not as if CURE hasn't been on my mind. I've continued receiving the newsletter (thank you). I really enjoyed the May 2018 issue. There was so much information packed into those few pages. Whoever edited the issue did a great job. The information was succinct but detailed.

Two things stood out to me. First, on page 8: Mayors and Criminal Justice Reform. Mayor Chokwe Lumumba's father, the late mayor of Jackson, MS, was my mentor and very close friend. So I just liked seeing his name. I haven't spoken to Mayor Lumumba since before I was segregated and transferred here last July.

More substantive though, on page 6: Are We Measuring the Right Thing? The questions asked (e.g., "Are we helping people convicted of crimes to form better relationships with their families and their law-abiding friends?" "Are we helping them to advance their educational skills?" ... "Are we helping them to respect others and to participate positively in civic and cultural life of their communities?") are poignant and necessary. In order to achieve different results, we must begin asking different questions.

It is important to ask these kinds of questions in order to change the trajectory of the dialogue, so what we hope becomes an indispensable component of the process of both learning and knowing.

I'm often surprised to discover that ideas that are probably "common sense" to you and me have never entered the thought processes of many of the men and women responsible for criminal justice and correctional policies. Not that they are bad people, but bureaucracy, expedience, the need for efficiency, and routine often leads to Group Think, which has the silhouette of common sense, but that's it. More voices. I'm always for more voices.

---

[*] MI-CURE is a grassroots justice reform organization. It is a chapter of National CURE. More info at https://www.mi-cure.org/

Quickly, on a personal level. I'm praying the newly formed Conviction Integrity Unit in Detroit helps me achieve some long overdue justice. They accepted the case for investigation. Hopefully this fall you will be introducing me as a speaker or dispatching me somewhere to contribute to fostering relationships that expedite the construction of a justice system worthy of our humanity and genius. Both as individuals and as a society.

Take care,
Lacino Darnell Hamilton

Dear Professor Shari,

It's been extremely difficult getting it in gear this morning. Just feel sluggish. The fit is tighter than usual. Big fish, little swamp. Sitting damn near in a squat position to type. Having no control over the temperature. A fan would be nice. Even a small one. It's muggy, sticky. I need to get more sleep. I'm only sleeping about four hours per night. That's really out of my control. The screaming and frustrated sounds from frustrated minds and throats never stops.

I'm listening to eighties and nineties R&B right now. Al B Sure, *In Effect Mode* ("Oooh This Love Is So"); Keith Sweat, *Make It Last Forever* ("How Deep Is Your Love"); *The Best of Atlantic Starr; The Best of Silk*; Karyn White; Shirley Murdock; Prince ("If I Was Your Girlfriend"). His music was authentic. I could listen to more up-tempo music to get going, but eighties and nineties R&B brings to mind memories of better days. I was free. Much younger (every few weeks I find a new gray hair in my beard). Life had its complications, but it didn't include micromanagement of my life.

When a cup of black coffee and the last era of good R&B doesn't do the trick, I talk to myself. People say there is nothing wrong with that as long as you don't answer back. Sometimes I'm in full blown conversation. "Lacino, what's the problem?" "I don't know?" "Snap out of it." "I'm trying." I prefer talking to myself to succumbing to monotony, idleness, or loneliness. What's crazy about that?

I'm listening to Shirley Murdoch right now, "Husband," on her album, *A Woman's Point of View*. If for no other reason, something is wrong with prison because there are no women and children. That's like living in a world with no sunshine, with no oxygen. This may be the cruelest part of prison. The prison was intended, according to a warden at the Ossining, New York, penitentiary: "In order to reform a criminal you must first break his spirit."[2] A world devoid of women and children might accomplish that. Why not reform through education? Through dialogue and partnerships?

Prisons have long been an extreme reflection of the American system itself: the stark life differences between rich and poor, the racism, the use of victims against one another, the lack of resources of the underclass to speak out, the endless "reforms" that change little. Dostoevsky once said: "The degree of civilization in a society can be judged by entering its prisons."[3] America can go to the moon, has first- and second-strike nuclear capacity, and can market anything but hasn't found ways to preserve and strengthen familial and communal bonds? Make that make sense.

Reform by eliminating sunshine and oxygen? Solving problems by breaking spirits? Reform through conflict and strife? Who's really crazy? All of which influence decision makers' understanding of justice and shape their response to harm. However, they run counter to the critical test of the genuineness of justice to the degree to which it commits itself to compassion and mercy, to restoration with harmony. The true function of justice is to evoke disclosures of love and wisdom, and to transform our life to make it a vehicle of that love and wisdom.

Keith Sweat, "A Right and a Wrong Way to Love Somebody," is not playing. He is singing about making love, but the words are appropriate. Why can't the American judicial system commit to a covenant of peace and the integrity of creation? This should be the goal no matter the offense: accountability, repentance (a radical change in directions), forgiveness, compassion, and reconciliation. Law does not have to be a process to punish or penalize. It can be a framework to teach people how to live a better life. It could be a healing process that restores good relationships among people or, if they do not have good relationships to begin with, foster and nourish an environment where good relationships can flourish. Radical, isn't it?

Last time I used the word "radical" over the phone, an incite to riot misconduct was written against me, and I spent almost ten months in solitary confinement. Imagine that? The message of compassion, love, and liberation is radical and has always come under assault. "What kind of man would leave you standing in the cold? He must have been a silly one to sacrifice a pot of gold." Those are the beginning words to Babyface's song, "Soon As I Get Home." I love love ballads. Each individual human being has unique value. Each individual human being is endowed with special qualities and talents. These concepts are central to the principles of justice. The basis for true happiness and contentment: spiritual. In what civilized world do people intentionally set out to break someone's spirit?

J. S. Auerbach, in *Justice Without Law* (1983), said of American society: "Law is our national religion; lawyers constitute our priesthood; the courtroom our cathedral, where contemporary passion plays are enacted."[4] Auerbach left out of this analogy that prisons are America's hell. Prisons and poverty. I don't know what redeems us though. What is our sacred text, our Torah, our Quran? American society doesn't seem to have avenues or mechanisms for redemption. Perhaps if it did I wouldn't have to work so hard to be exonerated—to be "born again."

I better go before this turns into a sermon. Hopefully you understand what I'm getting at? Only through working with one another can we put things back together when they fall apart. Justice measures success not in terms of numbers of cases solved or numbers of offenders imprisoned. Justice measures success by how much harm has been prevented or repaired. By how many relationships are restored. The path of retribution, of vengeance, can only dry up the soul of our country.

Your friend,
Lacino

Dear Professor Shari,

I don't know if you can tell, but I am a little embarrassed when people compliment me on being strong and resilient for how I have managed to self-educate and find ways to contribute to the movement for social justice despite being incarcerated all these years. I don't want you or anyone else to think that I don't go through it, because I do. I have cried my share of tears and find myself sitting with my head in my hands often. Not to mention that I have battled with various levels of depression the entire time I have been incarcerated.

I'm not implying that experiencing pain and strength are mutually exclusive, because they aren't, only that I don't want to be made into more than I am. I've really just been in survival mode all these years. Trying not to exit prison with quantities of emotional and psychological baggage that make me no good to myself or anyone else when released. On average that's how people exit prison, as a personal and social liability. I've really been fortunate to develop a sense of my own agency as well as a sense of social responsibility toward and with others, the society, and the broader world in which we live. And I wouldn't have been able to do it without the assistance of dozens of people, including yourself. Thank you.

Lacino

Dear Professor James A.,

You make a compelling argument, but I'm not sold. Many times in history people who are abused, who are at a material disadvantage, have been presented with the choice of keeping a low profile and hoping the abuse doesn't intensify. People have a tremendous threshold for pain, especially when they believe there is nothing they can do to stop the abuse. However, I choose to fight. It is not intelligent to hope someone or something causing harm will just stop, maybe feel regret and remorse.

Honestly, you are not supposed to understand how my refusal to follow rules helps me in the immediate or contributes to exoneration. Actually, they don't, not directly. But if I am going to be of use to others when released, I can't participate in my own demise. That's why I'm no fan of prison employment. Subsidizing my own incarceration? Hell no.

It is important not to separate the struggle for exoneration from the struggle for dignity and greater expressions of humanity. Not doing something simply because a tyrant orders me not to is never a legitimate reason not to do it. Even when the consequences are severe and certain, having the strength to resist is an accomplishment of Olympic proportions. It lets me know that economy of action and executive decision-making are still within my world of possibilities. It is good to know this and not just think it. A person can think what they want. Proving it is something different.

The idea that I can only pursue liberation by keeping a low profile is bullshit. I continue to acquire and develop a better understanding of true liberation by continuing to discover the connection between continuous capitulation on terms acceptable to my captors. Terms I find demoralizing: the forced appropriation of propaganda that I am inferior. Sometimes I'm rebellious just for the sake of being rebellious. Small acts of defiance may not liberate the body, as you say, but they do set examples of another way of doing things. They do open me to a range of options that translucent thoughts and wishful thinking never can.

This is where I part ways with others who have maintained they are innocent. This is where I differ even with people working to free me: who am I if I do not try to give meaning to my life outside the context of fear-based obedience? It is possible to enjoy qualitative independence in the here and now, not just when I get out.

If I am just happy to theorize about independence, it is just a superfluous awareness. A hallucination. A fabrication. But as long as I continue to set myself the task of living like a human being, right here, now, today, I can think and act without the prison pretending to be my brain.

The network of innocence clinics should think about what they ask men and women they work to exonerate. Why should I have to smile my way through abuse? I bet incarcerated men and women are the only victims of abuse this is asked of. No one would tell a woman being abused by a spouse or partner to "be good," don't "act out." If a child was being forced into a car of a stranger, we'd tell them to run, scream as loud as they can, call for help, kick, bite, scratch at their eyes, do whatever they have to do to bring attention to the situation so others can descend on the car and fuck that clown up, right? That's what I am doing. Except I've been pushed in already.

Even when the matter appears trivial (What is trivial when most everything has been taken?), acting in one's own best interest, I assure you, is worth the consequences. My choice not to go along to get along reflects political awareness and clarity that I am still a human being.

A log floating in water for ten years will not become an alligator, right? Well, being in prison, no matter how long the stay, I don't become mindless. And it doesn't make state-sponsored abuse legitimate. If people don't want to assist me because I refuse to "be good" in a bad situation, they don't understand it's about more than liberating my arms and legs and torso, but the complete me—body and mind.

Lacino

Rhonda,

So you're organizing a book club—that's great. You mentioned that your target participants are youths eight to fifteen years of age? That's such an important time in young peoples' cognitive and emotional development. The right books and structure for interrogating them will enable the members to learn about themselves in group-based social situations. I wish I'd had something like that to help me better understand all the changes that were taking place in my body and mind between those ages.

What have you done to prepare yourself to facilitate a book club? Before I was a member of the Michigan Theory Group, sponsored by the University of Michigan-Dearborn campus, my knowledge of group dynamics was limited. Well, limited might be an overstatement. The groups I was part of were formed on the streets of Detroit and based on selling crack cocaine. The central dynamic was violence, Black-on-Black violence.

Theory Group taught me that group settings provide opportunities to disclose attitudes, beliefs, and behaviors for the purpose of feedback and learning and that people don't have to make meaning alone. Too many young people are doing just that nowadays. They experience racism, classism (I think it's more accurate to use the word "class" instead of poor or poverty), all sorts of disadvantages due to a disproportionate concentration of wealth and power without the tools to interpret and analyze them. Literature provides young minds the opportunity to see themselves and the world in a broader context, and the opportunity for a more comprehensive grasp of systemic differentials to the conception and design of change efforts. You don't want them to just read, analyze, and leave it at that, right? A book club can be the beginning of group action.

Let me know if I can assist in any kind of way.

Lacino

Carl,

Each time you asked me to come up with a low-intensity activity that we can start to build awareness and support for prisoners, I thought to myself that there is nothing low intensity about these experiences. It took me a while to come around to the fact that low-intensity work is better than no work at all and that everything has to have a beginning. Seldom are those beginnings "high intensity."

Do you know how you can know something but sometimes need a reminder? Your letter got me to thinking about how developing social justice processes in a society and world steeped in oppression looks nothing like the fiction in many minds of that one right action that will reset the world. The seemingly smallest contradiction and most unlikely event or situation, if approached creatively, can help people develop the critical analytical tools necessary to understand oppression and their own socialization within oppressive systems. Literally anything can serve as a launching pad to develop a sense of agency and capacity to interrupt and change oppressive behaviors and interactions.

After thinking about all that you said in your last letter, what do you think about starting a book or movie club? Reading a book or watching a movie with a group of other readers and viewers and entering into dialogue is a collective experience. Readers and viewers become a community who are simultaneously exposed to the same experiences its pages and scenes provide. This is tantamount to a printed or cinematic rally. A major instrument of propaganda.

Although the term "propaganda" has a negative connotation, this derogation itself derives from propaganda. From the myth of impartial facts—both sides of the story—by which we are indoctrinated and pacified. To propagandize literally means to propagate one's own vision of reality and to disperse it among a community of readers, viewers, or listeners. Therefore a book or movie club can function as a continuous political process, one which propagates and organizes perspectives, defines new problems, new directions, and new solutions for its community.

I am aware this may come off as an oversimplification, but books and movies can help us make sense of, and hopefully, act more effectively against prisons appearing to be the only option to reduce or prevent harm. Whether a book or movie club expands, stays fixed, or dies depends on the ability to understand the awareness of its participants, respond to that awareness, and shape it further. Without such understanding, a book or movie club may very well amount to little more than a social gathering, not an instrument for change.

RECOMMENDED READINGS:
- *Soledad Brothers*, George L. Jackson
- *The Prisoner's Wife*, Asha Bandele
- *Are Prisons Obsolete?*, Angela Davis
- *It's About Time*, James Austin, John Irwin
- *Gates of Injustice*, Alan Elsner
- *The Real War on Crime*, Steven Donziger
- *Transcending*, Howard Zehr
- *Doing Life*, Howard Zehr
- *Crime and Punishment in America*, Elliot Curris
- *Code of the Street*, Elijah Anderson
- *The Soul Knows No Bars*, Drew Lader
- *Newjack*, Ted Conover
- *You Got Nothing Coming*, Jimmy Lerner
- *Violence*, James Gilligan
- *Preventing Violence*, James Gilligan

- *Lockdown America*, Christian Parenti
- *Women Doing Life*, Lora Bex Lampert
- *Locked Down, Locked Out*, Maya Schenwar
- *Invisible Punishment*, Mauer, et al.
- *Prisoner Once Removed*, Travis Waul
- *After Crime and Punishment*, Maruna, et al.
- *Inside Rikers*, Jennifer Wynn
- *In the Belly of the Beast*, Jack H. Abbott
- *Hard Times Blues*, Sasha Abramsky
- *Downsizing Prisons*, Michael Welch
- *Prison Masculinities*, Sabo, Kupers, London
- *Brothers and Keepers*, John E. Wildeman
- *Random Family*, Adrian LeBlanc
- *True Notebooks*, Mark Salzmen
- *Life Without Parole*, Victor Hassins
- *Life Sentences*, Wilbert Rideau
- *Committing Journalism*, Dennis Martin, Peter Suseman
- *Returning to the Teachings*, Todd Clear
- *Thinking About Crime*, James Q. Wilson
- *Fixing Broken Windows*, George Kelling, James Wilson
- *Illusion of Order*, Bernard E. Harcourt
- *Peacemaking Circle*, Kay Prenis
- *Women in Prison*, Kathryn Watterson
- *The Original Justice System and Woman*, B. Price

- *Laughing in the Dark*, Patrice Gaines
- *Couldn't Keep It to Myself*, Wally Lamb
- *A World Apart*, C. Rathbone
- *No Safe Haven*, Lori Girshick
- *In the Mix*, Barbara Owen
- *The Farm*, Andi Rierdon
- *Life on the Inside*, Jennifer Gonnerman
- *They Always Call Us Ladies*, Jean Harris
- *Inner Lives*, P. Johnson
- *The Women Who Couldn't Talk*, Susan McDougal
- *The Courage to Teach*, Parker Palmer
- *A Pedagogy of Liberation*, Ira Shor, Paulo Freir
- *Teaching to Transgress*, bell hooks
- *We Make the Road by Walking*, Myles Horton, Paula Freire
- *Total Confinement*, Lorna Rhodes

RECOMMENDED FILMS:

- *What I Want My Words to Do to You*
- *Mystic River*
- *Monster*
- *Dead Man Walking*
- *Murder in the First*
- *The Shawshank Redemption*
- *American History*

- *The Hurricane*
- *American Me*
- *Blood In Blood Out*
- *Brubaker*
- *Monster's Ball*
- *Somebody Has to Shoot the Picture*
- *Short Eyes*
- *An Innocent Man*
- *Birdman of Alcatraz*
- *Sleepers*
- *The Chamber*
- *Juvies*
- *Fight for Algiers*
- *A Prison Song*

Dear Lisa,

Have you ever read anything about the Fugitive Slave Act passed in 1850? It was a concession to southern states in return for the admission of stolen Mexican territories into the United States as nonslave states. The act made it easier for slave owners to recapture Blacks who escaped or simply kidnap Blacks and claim they had run away.

Northern Blacks organized resistance to the Fugitive Slave Act, denouncing President Millard Fillmore, who signed it into law, and Senator Daniel Webster, who was one of its most vocal proponents. One of those organizers was J. W. Loguen, son of a slave raped by her master. This is something the history books should point out more and stop calling those relationships romances or love affairs. Woman held in slavery were not in position to say no. The power dynamics were so imbalanced that if a woman held in slavery thought she was in love with her master, it should be attributed to Stockholm syndrome, not a true expression of deep and tender feelings.

J. W. Loguen escaped from the plantation, managed to go to and complete college, and became a minister in Syracuse, New York. The same year the Fugitive Slave Act was passed, he spoke at a meeting in Syracuse:

> The time has come to change the tones of submission into tones of defiance ... I received my freedom from heaven, and with it came the command to defend my title to it ... I don't respect this law. I don't fear it. I won't obey it. It outlaws me, and I outlaw it. I will not live a slave, and if force is employed to re-enslave me, I shall make preparations to meet the crisis as becomes a man. . . . Heaven knows that this act of noble daring will break out somewhere, and may God grant Syracuse be the honored spot, whence it shall send an earthquake voice through the land.[5]

The following year the chance came for Syracuse to be that spot. A runaway slave named Jerry was captured and put on trial. A crowd of

Blacks went to the courthouse where Jerry was held with a crowbar and a battering ram to break into the courthouse. Others had guns they used to hold the marshals at bay. They freed Jerry from the courthouse, and there is no record of him ever being captured again. I am not telling you to grab a crowbar and a battering ram (I am not telling you not to either), but your brother is in the same position as Jerry, the runaway slave.

Some people say it is hyperbole when prisons are referred to as modern-day slavery or a continuation of slavery. But it isn't. Have you ever interrogated the Thirteenth Amendment of the United States Constitution, ratified into law December 6, 1865, the same year chattel slavery was officially taken off the books?

Neither slavery nor involuntary servitude, except as a punishment for crime whereof the party shall have been duly convicted, shall exist within the United States, or any place subject to their jurisdiction.

I asked, have you ever interrogated that amendment? When it is read carefully, it becomes clear that slavery was never abolished. What was done is, stipulations were placed on who could be enslaved and that slavery would no longer be on plantations but in prisons. Where the Thirteenth Amendment reads neither slavery nor involuntary servitude *except* as punishment of a crime, it does not abolish slavery. The word "except" merely stipulates that slavery can only exist for the punishment of a crime.

People are confused about prison being slavery because they have been led to believe that there is only one kind of slavery, and that it involves plantations and picking cotton. However, the men who wrote the Thirteenth Amendment were not confused and obviously knew that once someone has been convicted of a crime, they could be forced back into a condition of slavery. The state plays the role of slave master and controls the lives of imprisoned men and women down to the minutest detail.

Your brother is like Jerry, a slave. Maybe not a cotton-picking slave, but he is a constitutional slave and he needs strategic and desperate support. He needs you to be an advocate for him of the J. W. Loguen variety. J. W. Loguen made his home in Syracuse a major station on the Underground Railroad. It is said that J. W. Loguen helped fifteen hundred escaping slaves on their way to Canada.

Slavery is viewed as legitimate because the state now controls it, because men and women appear to put themselves in prison. But if men can decide prison will be the new Black (i.e., slavery), it's not a leap that conditions like miseducation, a tight job market, and structural racism could have an influence on the growth of prisons on a scale the world has never before seen.

Just want to put this on the brain. Assisting your brother requires adding this into the equation. If not, you'll always come up short.

Your brother from another mother,
Lacino

Dear Amani,*

I called and spoke to a friend yesterday. He said I couldn't have called at a better time. He was logged onto your website and couldn't place where he knew your name from but was certain he knew it. When I called, it hit him—you are a friend of mine. Six degrees of separation. Are you familiar with that theory?

He logged onto Black and Pink Chicago, then a site referenced on their site, then a site referenced on that site, a couple more references and he was excavating his memory, digging for where he knew your name. He had nothing but compliments about your site, both content and setup.

When I returned to the tomb (cell), I reread your most recent correspondence. I thought long and hard about the poetry class you facilitated and the climatic poetry reading for the prisoners' population, guards, staff, and members of the public. I thought long and hard about my experiences with such spectacles and some observations I hope you will accept in the spirit in which they are shared.

There is an interesting arrangement between prisons and exhibition sport events, poetry readings, plays, and other theatrical performances. First, the performance is held in the newest or most sanitized performance space. Prisoner-painted murals cover the walls, floors have been scrubbed, sometimes freshly painted, and the smell of citrus wafts through. Why citrus I don't know, but it's the prison's fragrance of choice. I am certain someone was paid a lot of money to determine that citrus somehow best suits our bureaucratic management.

The dynamics of appearance and smell involve more than a simple contrast between display and reality (prisons are filthy and reek of trash and bodily fluids); these events suggest to the visiting audience that everything is all right on the inside. That prison can't be as awful as they have heard or imagine it is. The performance reinforces this charade.

---

* A young activist with whom Lacino corresponded.

The prisoner performers tend to be a group of "all stars" chosen by the prison because they fall outside the stereotype of what a prisoner is. This group usually gives themselves over to more reading, writing, and the development of artistic talents and skills than the general prisoner population. In exchange for being allowed to read their poetry or act out scenes from *Hamlet* or *Rent* or some other play that doesn't convey the misery in which we live, the prison and its staff receive a facelift. In this setting, with fellow prisoners and staff cheering the performers on, the totalitarian nature of the prison is obscured.

While these performances (you have to realize that's what they are, everyone from the guards at the front gate, staff in attendance, and prisoner audience are acting) are infrequent, when there is little else in terms of direct experience to measure prison practices, these performances hide that in other parts of the prison, sometimes just a few feet away, a variety of unusual human experiences (e.g., prolonged solitary confinement, naked persons living in their own excrement, solid steel doors leading to other solid steel doors, racial epithets, rigidly imposed rules) are underway.

Guards smile, staff shake hands and may give an impromptu speech blessing the performance, and prisoners in the audience with greased-up faces warned to be on their best behavior are all putting on a performance worthy of an Oscar. Actually, they are the real performers, not the prisoners reading poetry that made it through several layers of censorship. The excitement is genuine, but for different reasons. Guards and staff are excited they pulled things off. No major disturbances. Prisoners are excited to say hi to members of the public and consume beverages and light snacks reserved for these occasions. But everyone is essentially performing.

Of course there is always value in interaction between people on the outside and people on the inside. There is always value in progress that develops intellectual and artistic talents and skills. There is always value in events that counter stereotypes and false assumptions about the men and women inside American prisons. And there is always value in inter-actions between the inside and outside that could possibly lead to future interactions between the two groups. But my experiences as both an audi-ence member and a performer were always superseded by awareness that members of the public were being shielded from the real prison waiting for me as soon as the cheers and hand clapping ended.

The dirt. The grime. The smells that give me headaches. The meat that I cannot identify. The "get naked now and lay facedown on the ground." The "your opinion doesn't matter." You know, the real prison: the frustration. The anger. The despair. The depression. The monotony. The idleness. The loneliness. The always having to chase after some-thing. The always having to hide something. The always having to hold our ground against something or someone. The crying into pillows late at night. The births and graduations and weddings missed. The watch-ing children grow up through pictures, if one is lucky enough to receive pictures. The nieces and nephews you've never met and who may have never heard your name mentioned at a family function. The youthful appearance that has changed into lines across the forehead and graying hair. The sorries and apologies and remorse that are expressed a million times but never believed.

I hope this doesn't come off as me raining on your parade. I hope you continue going in and out of the lockup. Many of the men in your classes probably share some of these observations, but likely wouldn't share this with you for fear you couldn't handle it and wouldn't come back or wouldn't want you to think they are ungrateful. The best part of their week is when they know for certain you are coming and they are having class. They appreciate you beyond words. But this is part of that reality that can hopefully assist in you striking a balance between art and reality.

Your friend,
Lacino

Rhonda,

This is a positive development. I embrace the movement to eliminate bail bonds. Bail bonds have an utterly disproportionately negative impact on the poor. Things like loss of job, disruption in child care, inability to pay rent, and deeper destitution. Could you imagine spending a year in jail only because you can't afford bail, ultimately exonerated of all guilt, but your life is in ruins because you've been missing, essentially kidnapped and held for ransom? It happens all the time. Wealthy defendants can secure their freedom, no problem, don't have to worry about this.

Bail is determined by what people in the bail industry call risk assessment tools, algorithms. The purpose for these tools is to link pretrial detention to socioeconomic status rather than risk. That shouldn't come as a surprise; they replicate the biased assumptions of previous human decision makers. Some 11 million people are admitted to local jails annually, and on any given day, more than 730,000 people are being held—presumed to be innocent until proven guilty. The criminal justice system is effectively a system for keeping the poor in poverty while generating revenue to fund the criminal justice system.

Eliminating bail bonds is a major movement. This is not the solution to mass incarceration, and I'm increasingly pulling away from that term because mass incarceration or a little incarceration is a huge problem, but as we move forward, it will help keep people out of jail and out of prison. Find ways to support the movement even if it's just becoming more aware of what is going on so you can make others aware as well.

Miss you,
Lacino

"We need people who can articulate the struggle, who can come through the mud and represent us. . . . Most of those niggers are soldiers, just soldiers, revolutionary infantry. They're beautiful brothers, but they're rough. I have to do what I can to keep them in check. They don't know where it's headed, and they'll probably go down before we get to the starting line."

—Alprentice "Bunchy" Carter[6]

Dear Comrade,

You are an academic, an intellectual indisputably. But I think it is healthy for you to be in dialogue with brothers like myself for a change that can bring you back down to earth occasionally. You can sometimes get beside yourself with these "fresh perspectives" and different angles you come up with.

I am strongly against the idea of conflating crime with any sort of social justice consciousness or this idea that the system deems brothers like the one I wrote you about—that stabbed three prisoners—as threats. I believe this narrative you are pushing would ultimately do us a disservice on so many levels. It would give these brothers a crutch, a justification, and lend false legitimacy to their antisocial justice activities.

The only scenario of "crime" where this might make any sense is property crime in what groups like the BLA termed "appropriations," basically any attack on the system that chips away at its foundation and gives back to the people stolen from via deflated wages, inflated prices, interest payments larger than the principal, etc. And the only "criminals" that I see the system deeming as a threat are the Chamber brothers, Big Meech, Doc Holiday, Frank Lucas types. People who make *Fortune* 500 money. And this has more to do with the potential that it can be used to empower the community by building infrastructure, funding institutions, securing loyalty, and other activities of government. These young brothers that are wreaking havoc on other poor and oppressed people are more of a threat to themselves and to us than those who oppress them.

I am sure you are familiar with the concept of surplus population, right? Within the capitalist framework, it is inevitable for certain populations to be left out of profit sharing, that resources will be selectively apportioned, parts of society walled off (e.g., higher education), and so on. I argue that the system creates the conditions for these young brothers to resort to desperate acts of surviving, of trying to have some of the finer things in life, of adding some excitement to their predictable and boring lives. They go outside the system to satisfy their needs and wants not as a challenge to the system but because the system has pushed them out. Then the system can justify measures taken to push them back in. If you notice, the measures taken (stop and frisk, militarized schools, mass incarceration, etc.) push people into parts of the system where they can be controlled and/or incapacitated. The measures are never to share power, grow wealth, or include them in the decision-making process. Not choices but decisions—there is a huge difference.

Whenever a brother steals, robs, picks up a pistol, exploits members of the community, gives someone the death penalty, it is factored into capitalism. The states did not go on a prison-building spree in the late 1980s and 1990s before there were convictions to justify the building because construction companies had nothing better to do. Billions of dollars were appropriated to build prisons because social planners and policy makers were aware that some populations were going to be left out of the economic boom of the 1990s. They were aware that as the country transitioned from manufacturing to technology, those same populations were going to be left behind.

Prison is as American as apple pie. That is why America (despite only being 5 percent of the world's population) leads the world in imprisonment rates. America creates conditions where crime will flourish. For example, in here, administrators pretend to be against the gang culture that is steadily growing in size and influence, yet it does not take a proverbial rocket scientist to see gangism is actually promoted to divide and conquer.

Prison administrators prefer these reactionary kid groups over prison religions that were the primary organizing mechanism from the mid-1970s to the late 1990s because they promoted education, self-awareness, and militancy. Administrators know they can capitalize off the gangs that consist of historically oppressed people, poor, uneducated, mentally ill brothers who come from environments hostile to them. If they are able to pin the gang label on them, manufacture a threat, it gives them the moral high ground, justifies more jobs, more security, and a license to repress.

Steven Biko, who was the president of the South African Students' Organization from 1969 to 1972, and one of the leading architects of the Black Consciousness Movement in South Africa, spoke words that are pertinent here. He said that the brothers and sisters who appeared to be out of their minds had become shells of themselves, completely defeated, drowning in their own misery, a slave, an ox bearing the yoke of oppression with sheepish timidity. He said that it becomes necessary to see the truth as it is if we are to start any program designed to change the status quo.

The first step therefore is not to equate crime with social justice but to find ways to pump life back into these brothers' empty shells. To infuse them with pride and dignity. To remind them of their complicity in the crime of allowing themselves to be misused. We should not waste time constructing theories that lend legitimacy to crime. We have to figure out how to channel the pent-up forces of the angry masses to meaningful and directional opposition to the conditions that make so many of us criminals for just trying to live.

Lacino

Dear Comrade,

Both my parents are recovering crack addicts, catching very bad. They
are all in with a losing hand. They cannot even bluff their way to a win.
They have been catching bad for so long, what they say and do isn't
believable. But they cannot fold or cash out either; they owe too much to
all the wrong operations. They have to just hope their luck changes, but
it won't. Luck has nothing to do with the misery in which they live. Life
is about percentages and odds—complex calculus. They miscalculated so
long ago it will take too much of what they do not possess to go back and
correct their errors. Like many of their generation, and mine too, they
will have lived a life without having really lived at all.

Thinking about this is pretty overwhelming at times, but it is precisely
the extremes in which my parents sweat it out that create the urgency
to rise above the misery of the situation here. The barriers to social
intercourses with the outside world. A departure that is built right into
what cuts me off from you—locked doors, high walls, barbed wire, draw-
bridges, wooded areas. All aspects of life conducted in the same place
under a single authority. Every activity carried on in the immediate company of dozens of other men, all of whom are treated alike and required
to do the same thing together. All phases of the day's activities—which
there aren't many—tightly scheduled. The whole sequence of activities
being imposed from above by a system of explicit formal rulings and a
body of officials. It's all bad on my end also.

All these barriers and spheres of life mashed together presumably
help to maintain order, but do prison officials ever think about how this
will affect men and women when they are released from prison and have
to make choices for themselves? It is generally known that if an arm or
leg is bound so that it cannot be used, eventually it becomes unusable.
The same is true with intelligence. Prison induces and perpetuates the
very pathology which it claims to remedy. But this sort of contradiction
is not unique. To what extent are prisons substituting notions of behavior

modification for earlier notions of survival of the fittest, bell curve? To what extent do they offer acceptable and desired alibis for punishments that are largely applied to animals?

I will be home soon. And unlike tens of thousands of other men and women who want to put lots of distance between themselves and prison, who just want to forget, I won't. Prison is where I scratched out my first meaningful identity. A guide for thinking critically and thinking often. The place where I learned that no amount of pressure can prevent me from realizing a thought whose time has come. I owe a debt in the same way my parents do, except I cling to no ideations of bluffing or hoping luck makes the day. When those famous words are spoken—"All right, I will take over from here"—all bets are off and debts will be settled.

Lacino

Dad,

No matter how many times or how many ways I explain the past thirty-seven years of nonfulfillment, you never seem to understand. You definitely did not understand when I would come to you, thinking you would give me some fatherly advice. What father advises their son to "hustle harder?" To "get out and get it like you give?" Of course I listened to you because I looked up to you just that much. But you knew better than me the emotional and psychological and social reverberations. Sometimes I think you just did not care or had a peculiar way of showing it.

My life could have been very different. I had intellectual gifts even back then. But how could I think of anything other than the rent when you weren't thinking of it at all? I didn't understand back then why my teachers were so disappointed in my performance. They saw in me way back then what I see in myself today. What I am beginning to believe you simply refuse to see—A little Stokely, a little Patrice Lumumba, and a whole lot of moxie. It was very raw back then, but if you would have encouraged me to develop it, I would have.

I don't hold the past against you, but I will not pretend either. Where is the lesson in that? You weren't the best parent I needed you to be. Far from good at all. The lessons I learned in brothels and crack houses are not the sort of lessons a teenage boy should have been exposed to. And if you were teaching me the best of what you knew, shame on you. When you care about others, you strive to be and do better for them.

Not extraordinary, but at least the basics: a roof, food in the fridge, watch a Pistons game together every once and again. But you couldn't do that. That girl was more important than me. You gave her all your thought, all your energy, all that you managed to scrape and claw for. There is no solace in being a distant second.

But that was a long time ago. Now people come to me for advice. I help them understand that they are not marginal, the opposite of how you made me feel. I encourage people to participate in the transformation

244

that is taking place all around the country. Often in small but significant ways. You encouraged me to be part of the chaos.

No matter how frustrated I am with you at times, I'm still convinced you are capable of looking critically at the world in a dialogical encounter with others. That's the beauty in what I'm helping to build. It's not just for those with the most money or the most education. It's for everyone. I love you.

Lacino Darnell H.

Dear Myra,*

I woke up in a foul mood—it was all a dream.

We were on the south coast of West Africa, in Ghana. Strolling up Chokwe Lumumba Boulevard. Named after my mentor and friend, the late Jackson, Mississippi, mayor and civil rights icon. We were having such a good time talking, laughing, taking in the sites. Eating shea nuts, bananas, and cassava bread. It was as if the past twenty-four years of bullshit separating you and me never happened. You saw me and I saw you. Saw the joy, the pain, so many possibilities. You are without a doubt one of my favorite people.

Foul mood because the same two fools that were shouting and screaming about a lot of nothing when I dozed off a couple hours ago, their shouting came in-between the closest I have been to you in far too long. It was as if they entered the dream just to be disruptive.

Prison has always been a place where broken people meet up, but the people here have never been shattered. Prison has descended into something awfully frightening. Prison is a clown show, of all ages and races. A daycare center for wannabe gang bangers. Guys who get respect and gain reputations over acting against the most vulnerable prisoners. It has become the norm to be ignorant, have no agenda, play all day, be loud, be a pill head, and jump from one gang to another. Even the religions operate like gangs nowadays.

When I first entered the prison system, I used to look forward to seeing the religious brothers when we went to recreation. I used to anticipate getting my hands on new books, having rigorous debates, being challenged to be my best self. I know much of the change in these groups come from inertia and stagnancy, little or no progress, but there is also a lack of interest, apathy, and intrigue with education. A lot of giving up. This in turn makes the existing barriers even more intolerable. Accelerates impatience

---

* A childhood friend of Lacino's.

and the lowering of the threshold of frustration toward failure. Failure reinforces the sense of personal and group powerlessness.

I am so disgusted with this environment on a day-to-day basis. Most of the time, I just stay to myself. I wouldn't go outside for that one hour each day to stretch my legs if I did not have to use the phone. I cannot recall how many times a day I hear ignorant shit like, "I'm never going to change," "What is reading going to do for me?" "I was born a nigga, I am going to die a nigga." It's all ignorance and fear, I tell you. Scared the guy who is just as scared as they are, but doesn't show it, is going to think they are weak, a sucker, and talk down to them. But what is weaker than not having a meaningful identity, purpose, direction, something worthy of living for instead of always talking about what one is willing to die for? So many of these guys are caught in the paradox of prison, unable to resolve their personal conflicts either in positive or in direct and assertive antisocial behavior.

I thought writing to you would lighten the mood. It hasn't. I am going to lay back down and try to catch back up with your beautiful smile and laugh that makes me want to laugh.

Lacino

Dear Professor James A.,

When your letter arrived, I was sitting on the edge of the bunk, pissed. I don't get why guards demand head nods and smiles and outward signs of "sincere" appreciation for doing things required of them and within their job description (fucking me over). The shit borders on sadism, masochism, or both. They expect me to thank them for their role in bending and twisting me in all sorts of unnatural shapes so that I will fit into this unnatural space. This is like *Fifty Shades of Gray*, except I do not consent and there is no safe word to make them stop.

I'm supposed to thank someone for treating me like I don't matter the least bit. I'm supposed to get down on my knees and salute the uniform. "You don't know how to say thank you Hamilton?" What is it with Americans and prostrating toward uniforms? The man or woman in the uniform can be a real piece of shit, but if they don the right uniform, I'm supposed to get on my knees and sing their praise because I am forced to wear this monkey suit. The guard wanted me to thank him for giving me a food tray where the bread, cake, beets, gravy, and Kool-Aid were all mixed together. "I didn't have to give you dinner at all." Dig that.

Uniforms are another form of identity politics. Don't think for one second "prison guard" isn't an identity. Like Nazis or Klansmen. But since the prison guard identifies with a hierarchical relationship in which dominant and privileged groups reap advantage from the disempowerment of Blacks, women, immigrants, poor whites, and gays and lesbians (targeted identities), conservatives are silent. It's not that they are against identity politics, as long as we identify with dominant and privileged groups or symbols of their dominance or privilege. What they are against is targeted identities uniting and struggling for power sharing and resources. It's easier to dominate individuals than to dominate cohesive groups.

How people come out of prison and interact with the wider society cannot be fully understood without acknowledging that guards' active aim is our compliance in both action and spirit. Prison is not just a physically restricting structure but restrictions forced into the human psyche as well. The spirit and inward feelings with which I go about my day is an official concern. Dig that, too.

On further thought, I do get why guards demand head nods and smiles and outward signs of appreciation toward them, because they do not see me (or any other incarcerated person) as an individual. To them I am just an appendage of the prison. Like a cell or a barbed-wire fence. No personality. No ability to think for myself, or feel. All I am supposed to do is what I'm told, and that includes being told how to feel. I want to throw that tray at him when he comes back to get it. And when he's standing there wearing the tray, I should tell him, "I didn't have to give you the tray at all." Then I'd nod and smile. Hurt myself smiling so hard. I might even salute him.

Lacino

Dear Maya,

Thank you for writing. You are such a great friend and always seem to know exactly what to say to lift my spirits.

Nothing has changed here, I am still in solitary confinement. And well, I am doing about as good as can be expected under the circumstances. Actually, risking understatement, I am buried alive inside Marquette's maximum security prison.

I am locked in a windowless cell measuring ten by eight feet, twenty-four hours per day. For one hour every other day, I am handcuffed, chained around the waist, and allowed exercise and a shower in a small cage. I am not allowed to interact with others or to participate in any educational, vocational, or employment programs. All meals are delivered to the cell. I have no access to a phone. And while I am permitted two one-hour non-contact visits per month—always conducted through glass—Marquette is 455 miles away from my hometown of Detroit. Opportunities to visit family and friends are rare.

For all intents and purposes, I am dead to everything but melancholic anxieties and horrible despair. This is torture.

I have existed under these conditions for over seven months with no prospects of release in the near future. The system here is rigid, strict, and hopeless solitary confinement. It is not natural or humane to be isolated like this day after day, month after month. Actually, it has long been known by those who research and labor to abolish solitary confinement that even a relatively brief exposure of time to severe environmental restrictions and social interactions has a profoundly deleterious—often catastrophic—effect on mental functioning. In such situations people often descend into a mental torpor or "fog," in which alertness, attention, and concentration all become impaired.

All day and night I can hear the madness coming from the throats of men who cannot take it anymore, frustrated souls from behind the bars of each cell, reaping rackets from the walls, the hollow vibrations from sink and toilet combined into one. Our iron beds are bolted to the floor. Lights are never turned off. These things take on frightening significance. They result in loss of appetite, insomnia, irritability, emotional withdrawal, depression, paranoid ideation, and easily provoked anger, which may escalate into "acting out."

Several guys on my tier have argued the last three days—promising to kill each other if the opportunity ever presents itself—over a pair of socks that came up missing in the laundry. This type of thing happens all the time. Of course, the inability to shift attention away from something as trivial as a pair of missing socks is not the worst of it. Many of the men here with me smear themselves with feces. They mumble and scream incoherently all day and night. They descend into the horror of self-mutilation, some eating parts of their bodies.

My first couple of weeks in solitary, an older white gentleman in a wheelchair who repeated over and over again how bored he was hanged and killed himself on a dare. The frequency with which these acts of despair and hopelessness occur should attract administrative as well as clinical concern but rarely do. The guy in the cell next to me and a guy around the corner both recently attempted suicide.

Not all people locked down in solitary confinement react precisely in these manners. In some, the trauma and harms are less conspicuous. In others, dejection and utter despondence set in earlier, or later. But none are unaffected. Not anyone. Not me. The challenges of writing under the tensions and hostilities created by social and sensory deprivation cannot be shrugged off. To encourage myself, I repeat out loud the words of Viktor E. Frankl: "Life holds meaning under any condition—even the most miserable ones."[7] I try to believe this.

Before writing, I strip the sheets and blanket from the refurbished piece of corrugated rubber that masquerades as my mattress, then fold it in half to serve as a writing surface. I do the same with a pillow that differs from the so-called mattress only in size, except it is used to cushion my knees. Kneeling is the most comfortable position from which to write.

I take several deep breaths, wipe the cold perspiration from my face, and go through a series of knuckle cracking and hand exercises. Writing with a three-inch rubber "security pen" causes my hands to cramp and swell. The pain is both excruciating and debilitating. I feel like giving up before getting started.

Prison administrators justify the use of all sorts of security methods, of which solitary confinement is the central pathogenic technique, by claiming the prison's need to modify aggressive behavior, reduce tension, make prisoners more obedient, and rehabilitate recalcitrant prisoners. However, those justifications do not match the reality. How is making prison smaller, narrower, and more confined going to reduce tensions? It is far more likely that solitary will not only place people at risk for greater anxiety and stress but also lead to lasting negative changes. These include persistent symptoms of post-traumatic stress (such as flashbacks, chronic hypervigilance, and a pervasive sense of hopelessness) and a continuing pattern of intolerance of social interaction.

All of these deep issues make people more susceptible to recidivism. The same way over two-thirds of people released from prison are rearrested in the first three years, a high percentage of prisoners released from solitary confinement quickly return. After people are released from solitary confinement, the trauma they experienced often prevents them from successfully readjusting to the environment of the "general population" in prison and perhaps even more significantly, often severely impairs their capacity to reintegrate into the broader community on release.

My friends write and ask how I am holding up. I always reply, "Just fine." While sincere in my response, I wonder if that is true, or even possible. No one here openly acknowledges the psychological harm or stress experienced as a result of the stringent conditions under which we're placed. I believed the reluctance to acknowledge this harm is a response to the perception that solitary confinement is an overt attempt by administrators and guards to "break us down." If we fully acknowledge that solitary is the product of an arbitrary exercise of power (rather than the fair result of a reasonable process), it can be even more difficult to bear.

What is important to note is not only that we as prisoners are often extremely fearful of acknowledging the psychological stress and harm we experience behind these walls, but that administrators and guards are fearful of doing so too. The consequences of caging people causes damage to both jailed and jailer. This is a point that has to be emphasized more often—all who exist or work in this environment are affected. Prison solves no social problems; it merely creates new and more complicated ones. It is a descending spiral ending in emotional and psychological harm for all.

My friends also write and ask how they can aid me. Books and letters help break up the monotony, loneliness, and idleness. But I recognize my experience as a social experience, not an individual sort of thing, and so I ask that in aiding "me," they do not embrace the "spokesperson" model of concern about solitary confinement. Isolating specific exemplary cases will not bring justice. That model tends to emphasize the individual rather than the collective injury. It dismantles collective responses and diverts attention from the larger picture: solitary confinement is a form of torture. And every day, in every state, many thousands of people in American prisons are tortured with little recognition or outrage.

My friends, or anyone for that matter, can assist the fight against solitary by becoming more informed that torture not only functions in countries where leaders elect themselves but routinely in our country, under the cover of criminal justice. Become more informed about how torture operates in American prisons through normalizing security techniques that are then taken as a given. Just being more informed is likely to bring up the question, "In whose interest does the system of social and sensory deprivation operate?" Asking who benefits and who pays helps to expose our collective lack of imagination when it comes to dealing with problems, pursuing accountability, and determining what actions should be taken to meet the needs of victims.

I hope what I write resonates. Solitary confinement is a tragic problem. It's also terrifying. When you are suffering like we are suffering, you simply cannot imagine that nobody will come along to stop the pain. And when no one does, the temptation to choose death over despair, for many, is overwhelming. Make no mistake: solitary confinement is torture.

Lacino Darnell Hamilton

Lisa,

I know the statistics off the top of my head: we are two and a half times more likely than whites to be living in poverty, our babies are three times more likely to die as infants, our unemployment rate is double that of whites, we typically only earn eighty cents for every dollar earned by white counterparts, our household earnings are less, our incarceration rates are about seven times that of whites, and so on and so on. These statistics can only be explained by long-standing structural white supremacy. Do you follow?

Yes, all individuals are morally responsible for their individual actions. However, when something happens over and over again over a long period of time, it's bigger than personal bias. It's the historical narrative, it's law, it's economic policy, it's social customs, it's educational practices, it's a web of relationships and structures that shade nearly all aspects of our society. Call individuals out, correct them accordingly, but don't lose sight of the proverbial forest for the trees.

Lacino Hamilton

Dear Dr., Professor, friend of mine,

I am in receipt of the three essays. I asked several other people before asking you to send them. None had success finding them. I really did not expect you to either. I am thankful you did. I promise to get all I can from them and in return produce something worthy of your search. Once again, thank you.

To what extent are we responsible for what happens to us while incarcerated? That is such a broad question. I will isolate what I think you are asking, depart from there, and you redirect me if I miss the mark, okay?

In the early 1990s, Atiba Shanna published a series of articles in *Crossroads* on the responsibilities of oppressed groups, specifically the responsibility of prisoners. He asked the same question you asked me, except he posed it to a much larger audience. I read those articles as a frustrated twenty-one-year-old in my second year of incarceration. I had the opportunity to reread them a few months ago after turning forty-three. They have retained their force and relevance.

The first time I read them, it surprised me, as I had not thought more deeply about this before then. Growing up in the midst of deindustrialization, the 1980s crack attack, and an unprecedented prison expansion, it seemed like every few months someone from the neighborhood was being sentenced to prison. Chances were, I was going to spend some time there, too. But growing up, it never occurred to me I possessed the responsibility or the capacity to determine the outcome of anything bigger than me.

It wasn't just that I was physically small, but back then I thought small. I thought in squares. I did not know anything about thinking outside the box. It simply never entered my mind that I could do anything about the people, places, or systems that seemed so much more powerful than myself. Sure, I was running through the neighborhood trying to control a few apartment buildings, a city block here or there, but the police, the courts, the prison system? Not only did I think small, think in squares, but there was some cowardice somewhere in the equation.

For the first time, with Atiba's question ringing in my mind, it really hit me that it is not possible to have all my liberties stripped from me, be treated like a mindless being, and return home unscathed if I did not assume greater responsibility for myself and sometimes assume responsibility for those around me. No one who always has to chase after something, always has to hide something, or always has to hold their ground against something—or someone—is going to come out of this unharmed if they don't build some sort of an offense.

I just had it in my mind that I was going to be all right. That I was "real." What more could be required than that? But Atiba didn't just ask the question, he quite properly turned the question back to prisoners and asked what our responsibilities are to ourselves. His articles got me thinking how systems of oppression are designed with the "real" ones in mind. That if the rebellious and recalcitrant types could become incapable of maintaining an adequate state of alertness, attention, and concentration, then those with less will power and determination would definitely succumb, be scathed, and as a friend of mine likes to say, be "through with money."

Atiba got me thinking how in some situations just being "real" isn't enough. If I was going to do more than just survive, which should not be the goal, but if I was going to acquire greater capacity to take control of the situation here, or any other situation, I was going to have to rebuild myself. And rebuild to win.

I'm aware the word "privileged" is not usually associated with people in prison. However, people in prison do have the privilege, the leisure, and on rare occasion the facilities to grow and develop into an archetype, the privilege (at least while they are inside) not to have to deal with the day-to-day grind of trying to keep up with the rent or just trying to keep things from falling apart and turn nearly all of our attention and energy toward solutions. Long-term, short-term, in whole, in part, acceptable, and some solutions that aren't widely accepted and for which only history can judge. As horrible as prison is, there are some limited privileges.

Perhaps the most well-known example of someone who turned nearly all their attention and concentration toward solutions was Malcolm X. Just consider his transformation from street hustler to international icon. He developed a process where he studied ideas for their relevance to his life and those similarly situated. During that process he no longer took ideas to mean what others said they meant. He realized that he possessed the capacity to determine the outcome of larger social and political happenings.

What prison was designed to accomplish was of no consequence. Malcolm X realized his responsibility as much deeper than keeping his nose clean in order to persuade the parole board to grant release. Something I wish my parents understood. I mean, of course release is an important part of every imprisoned person's life. The probability of release is fractional if we do not meet parole board recommendations. But Malcolm X's ultimate responsibility was to be and do his very best. He proposed that the prison model of isolation and monotony and the manufacturing of all sorts of tensions were inferior to finding purpose and direction.

Malcolm X was not from another planet. He was a street hustler who did not advance past the eighth grade. But once in prison, once he began to expand control over his thoughts, it led to a corresponding contraction of others' control over how he saw the world and his place in it. This inevitably resulted in Malcolm X returning to society as both an asset to himself and others. So if Malcolm X can be used as an example (there are others): to what extent are we responsible for what happens to us while in prison? We are completely responsible.

We owe an obligation to seek understanding of the forces that control our lives and to which we respond. A responsibility to use every resource and strength in an effort for clarity and perspective. Then we can do more than hold other oppressed people hostage in a few apartment buildings or on the block. We can begin the difficult work of abolishing police, courts, and prisons and build something in their place that in transformative ways addresses harm and strengthens community accountability in ways that include both the person who was harmed as well as the person who committed the harm. Some real justice.

Just before I forget, I don't get down with the idea of someone who has someone paying their debt by being warehoused in prison. A debt may very well be owed, but it can only be paid by returning to the place and among the people where the harm was committed and repairing what has been damaged or restoring what has been lost. This has to be included in our responsibilities.

Tell me what you think of this and, how Atiba Shanna posed this question to a much larger audience, how we can do the same.

Lacino Darnell Hamilton

RECOMMENDED READING

During the writing of his letters, Lacino Hamilton read with intense focus to access and use the tools of struggle and liberation his political and spiritual ancestors developed. However, the books and articles came to him piecemeal as did his writing during his twenty-six years of imprisonment. For this reason, Hamilton has cited the list of books that guided him during this time for readers to begin their abolitionist endeavors. The books, listed below, mark the beginnings of his scholarship and hopefully your own.

- ◆ *Soledad Brothers*, George L. Jackson
- ◆ *The Prisoner's Wife*, Asha Bandele
- ◆ *Are Prisons Obsolete?*, Angela Davis
- ◆ *It's About Time*, James Austin, John Irwin
- ◆ *Gates of Injustice*, Alan Elsner
- ◆ *The Real War on Crime*, Steven Donziger
- ◆ *Transcending*, Howard Zehr
- ◆ *Doing Life*, Howard Zehr
- ◆ *Crime and Punishment in America*, Elliot Curris
- ◆ *Code of the Street*, Elijah Anderson
- ◆ *The Soul Knows No Bars*, Drew Lader
- ◆ *Newjack*, Ted Conover
- ◆ *You Got Nothing Coming*, Jimmy Lerner
- ◆ *Violence*, James Gilligan

- *Preventing Violence*, James Gilligan
- *Lockdown America*, Christian Parenti
- *Women Doing Life*, Lora Bex Lampert
- *Locked Down, Locked Out*, Maya Schenwar
- *Invisible Punishment*, Mauer, et al.
- *Prisoner Once Removed*, Travis Waul
- *After Crime and Punishment*, Maruna, et al.
- *Inside Rikers*, Jennifer Wynn
- *In the Belly of the Beast*, Jack H. Abbott
- *Hard Times Blues*, Sasha Abramsky
- *Downsizing Prisons*, Michael Welch
- *Prison Masculinities*, Sabo, Kupers, London
- *Brothers and Keepers*, John E. Wildeman
- *Random Family*, Adrian LeBlanc
- *True Notebooks*, Mark Salzmen
- *Life Without Parole*, Victor Hassins
- *Life Sentences*, Wilbert Rideau
- *Committing Journalism*, Dennis Martin, Peter Suseman
- *Returning to the Teachings*, Todd Clear
- *Thinking About Crime*, James Q. Wilson
- *Fixing Broken Windows*, George Kelling, James Wilson
- *Illusion of Order*, Bernard E. Harcourt
- *Peacemaking Circle*, Kay Prenis
- *Women in Prison*, Kathryn Watterson
- *The Original Justice System and Woman*, B. Price
- *Laughing in the Dark*, Patrice Gaines
- *Couldn't Keep It to Myself*, Wally Lamb

- *A World Apart*, C. Rathbone
- *No Safe Haven*, Lori Girshick
- *In the Mix*, Barbara Owen
- *The Farm*, Andi Rierdon
- *Life on the Inside*, Jennifer Gonnerman
- *They Always Call Us Ladies*, Jean Harris
- *Inner Lives*, P. Johnson
- *The Women Who Couldn't Talk*, Susan McDougal
- *The Courage to Teach*, Parker Palmer
- *A Pedagogy of Liberation*, Ira Shor, Paulo Freir
- *Teaching to Transgress*, bell hooks
- *We Make the Road by Walking*, Myles Horton, Paula Freire
- *Total Confinement*, Lorna Rhodes